JULIA BUCKROYD first trained and practised as an historian of 17th century Scotland at the universities of St Andrews, McMaster, Ontario, Cambridge and Oxford. In her mid-thirties she retrained first as a counsellor at Birkbeck College, University of London, and then as a psychotherapist with the Guild of Psychotherapists. This training was in the field of psychoanalytic counselling and psychotherapy, but she has since read widely in other counselling traditions and would now describe herself as an integrative or pluralist therapist. She values the huge development of knowledge and understanding which has exploded across the psychotherapeutic world with the development of attachment theory, the growth of neuroscience, the advances made by body therapies, the vastly increased sophistication of approaches to trauma and the advances made by cognitive therapies. Her work in the field of disordered eating attempts to make use of all these influences.

Her first job as a counsellor, 1984–1989, was as Student Counsellor at London Contemporary Dance School (LCDS). It was there that she first became interested in disordered eating. She then worked full time in private practice, working mostly with people with disordered eating, from 1990 until 1994.

From 1994–2008 Julia Buckroyd was employed at the University of Hertfordshire (UH) where from 1999 she increasingly undertook research in the fields of eating disorders and obesity. In 2002 she was made Professor of Counselling. In this role she established the Obesity and Eating Disorders Research Centre at UH. Since 2008, as Emeritus Professor of Counselling, she has continued to develop these ideas and lectures and conducts workshops widely throughout the UK.

Julia Buckroyd has written two programmes (with manuals) which incorporate her understanding of disordered eating. The first, Weight Management for Seriously Obese People, has been developed for use in the NHS for patients with a BMI of 35 or more. Further details can be obtained from the author. The second is a programme for the general public called Understanding Your Eating which offers courses to those troubled by their eating behaviour. More can be read about this programme in the resources chapter of this book and on the website http://www.understandingyoureating.co.uk.

Understanding Your Eating
How to eat and not worry about it

Julia Buckroyd

Open University Press

Open University Press
McGraw-Hill Education
McGraw-Hill House
Shoppenhangers Road
Maidenhead
Berkshire
England
SL6 2QL

email: enquiries@openup.co.uk
world wide web: www.openup.co.uk

and Two Penn Plaza, New York, NY 10121-2289, USA

First published in Great Britain in 1989 by Macdonald Optima.
Revised edition published in 1994 by Optima.
Second edition revised published in 1996 by Vermilion, an imprint of Edbury
Press.
This edition published 2011

A catalogue record of this book is available from the British Library

ISBN-13: 978-0-335-24197-2
ISBN-10: 0-335-24197-2
eISBN: 978-0-335-24198-9

Library of Congress Cataloging-in-Publication Data
CIP data applied for

Typeset by RefineCatch Limited, Bungay, Suffolk
Printed and bound by CPI Group (UK) Ltd, Croydon, CR0 4YY

The **McGraw-Hill** Companies

Praise for this book

"Symptoms of disordered eating are fantastically common. Which one of us doesn't have a worry about weight or shape, or try to diet at some stage or another? Even if one's symptoms don't add up to a formal eating disorder they can still cause a lot of misery, worry and difficulty maintaining a steady, healthy weight. This valuable book offers meaning and makes sense of how food and eating may be misused and become entangled with emotions as a way of dealing with them. The book offers up to date, specialist advice based on years of clinical practice, coupled with an outline of the research in the field. The subject is enlivened for the reader by inviting them to engage in self-reflective exercises- 'light bulb' moments- and identify with their own issues. Julia Buckroyd brings all this together in a highly readable and digestible book. I will recommend it to all of my clients and to many people outside my clinic."

—Dr Helena Fox - Clinical psychiatrist for Channel 4's
Supersize Vs Superskinny and for the eating disorders
unit at Capio Nightingale Hospital

"To understand your eating you first have to understand yourself. This easily-read book helps you to step back and comfortably discover who you are and what might influence your eating habits. For an individual with problems eating, or for the health professional who needs to understand more, this book can open the window and shed a very bright light."

—Dr Ian Campbell - Founder of the National Obesity
Forum and medical consultant on ITV's
The Biggest Loser and Fat Chance

"I really enjoyed this book. It certainly mirrors my approach to help people understand where their eating difficulties have come from. I think it will be a really valuable resource for those trying to improve their relationship with food. It offers insight in a very straightforward and readable way. I can certainly see myself recommending it to my clients."

—Ursula Philpot, on-screen dietician for Channel 4's
Supersize Vs Superskinny and senior lecturer
at Leeds Metropolitan University

"The question of how to develop a healthy relationship with food and eating is a major challenge for many individuals. This book is highly recommended for anyone who is interested in the meaning of food and eating, in learning why diets do not work, and in understanding what is required to move on from destructive patterns of eating. Julia Buckroyd writes in an accessible, friendly style, with many fascinating case examples from her own practice. It is essential reading for people who struggle with their use of food, for those who share their lives, and for practitioners who have professional involvement with this topic."

—Professor John McLeod, Professor of Counselling
at the University of Abertay Dundee

Contents

Part III

For my clients and supervisees,
who have taught me almost everything I know.

Acknowledgements

In the more than 20 years that have gone by since the first version of this book was published I have been on a continuous learning curve. Many people have contributed to my developing understanding of disordered eating. I would like to acknowledge some of them here.

For five years, from 2002 to 2007, Sharon Rother and I had a most productive and stimulating research relationship, from which emerged two books and a number of papers. Much of the research and clinical experience of disordered eating has come from group programmes that I developed around that period. There have been some outstanding group leaders whose work has greatly contributed to the growth of my understanding of obesity, including Carol Bush, Jo Coker, Sue George, Carole Green and Diane Redfern.

Janet Biglari and Sevim Mustafa have advanced my knowledge and understanding of bariatric surgery and its psychological implications. I look forward to ongoing clinical and research connections.

I have learned much from my research students in the area of disordered eating, especially Sarah Barnett and Deborah Seamoore. Similarly, my supervisees have kept me thinking with their presentation of client work, especially Marian Brindle, Jenny Heron and Deborah Meddes.

I value the contribution to my work from colleagues in related fields, especially Dr Jean Hughes in the field of dietetics and Dr Nick Troop for his knowledge of eating disorders and statistical expertise.

I am grateful to the University of Hertfordshire for the ten years in which I was permitted to continue my researches in disordered eating and given the opportunity to establish a research centre for obesity and eating disorders. This generous support enabled me to carry out a number of research projects and to formulate the ideas that are described in this book.

I am extremely grateful to all the clients over more than 25 years who have entrusted me with their stories and from whom I have learned almost everything I know. Some of the client examples are taken directly from the earlier versions of this book. All those cases had specific permission from the people concerned, and the details have been changed to prevent identification. New examples are put together from a range of different clients, so that no one example refers to any single person. Still, they refer to real people and reflect some of the many circumstances in which people feel the need to use food to help them manage their lives.

Preface

An earlier version of this book was published as *Eating Your Heart Out* (1989)[1] based on the work that I undertook at London Contemporary Dance School (LCDS) between 1984 and 1989. A second edition in 1996 incorporated a further five years of work with people with disordered eating in private practice. In this earlier form the book generated many positive responses from reviewers and readers. Since it has been out of print a number of people have urged me to prepare a new edition. This current version of the book, however, is more than a new edition of *Eating your Heart Out*; it is a revisiting of my understanding of eating disorders, hence its new title, *Understanding your Eating*. At the time of the first edition I had recognised that eating disorders were often the result of earlier emotional trauma. In the years since *Eating your Heart Out* was first published in 1989 there have been tremendous advances in the understanding of the importance of childhood experience for later life – those developments collectively known as 'attachment theory'. This rewritten version of the book explores the implication of these theories for an understanding of eating disorders. I now argue that eating disorders are indeed a response to emotional trauma, but that they are characteristic of those whose early experience has not prepared them adequately to deal with life's difficulties and who therefore find themselves using food as a means of emotional regulation. I am indebted to the pioneering work of neuroscientists and attachment theorists for this understanding, especially Allan Schore, Daniel Stern, Peter Fonagy and their interpreters, particularly Sue Gerhardt.[2]

A second major change in this version of the book is my use of the growing consensus that much eating behaviour that is not formally diagnosable as an eating disorder nevertheless causes great distress to many people. I have indicated that I wish the book to encompass the problems of this wider group by the use of the phrase 'disordered eating'.

The third major change is the incorporation within this version of the very substantial amount of research that suggests that almost half of those who are obese have a relationship with food that can only be called disordered. This was earlier partly recognised by the inclusion of the term 'binge eating disorder' within the field of eating disorders, but has not been accompanied by a more general attempt to offer psychological understanding to those who are significantly overweight. I hope that this book will do something to correct that situation.

Part I

Introduction

This book is for people who are concerned about their eating behaviour because they feel it is beyond their control. I call this behaviour 'disordered eating', whatever form it takes. You may not have a diagnosable 'eating disorder', but if you are upset by your eating behaviour this book may be of use to you. With so much inexpensive food about, lots of us are eating more than we should and many of us are trying to undo the effects by dieting or trying to moderate our eating behaviour. Others are perpetually anxious about their weight, shape and size and are involved in an endless battle with their need for food. Many of us know that our food choices are not good for our health but find it difficult to improve our diet. Many of us have learned how to count calories; we mostly know what we should eat, even if we don't, and many of us spend quite a lot of our lives worrying about having eaten too much. Unfortunately, these worries are very common in a culture where there is more food than we have ever had available to us before. For most of human history – indeed all of it until about the 1960s – food has been a scarce and valuable resource. In the past 50 years, for advanced western economies, it has become cheap and everywhere available. As populations we have generally found that change hard to manage. In the UK most of us are now overweight.

Many people have the difficult experience that although they know exactly what they should be eating, they can't manage to follow their own good advice. Many people are also constantly preoccupied by anxieties about food, weight, shape and size, to the point that these worries interfere with their everyday functioning and their enjoyment of life. This is different from the ordinary anxieties of those who are simply concerned to exercise a little self-discipline. These more troubled people fall into roughly three groups: the first is those who don't eat enough, out of anxiety about eating too much and getting fat; the second is those who eat too much and then take action to undo the effects, for instance, by vomiting or purging or starving; the third is those who once they start to eat can't stop, who don't succeed in undoing the effects and therefore become overweight or even very fat. This book is written for those three groups of people. It is also written for people whose eating behaviour seems strange and worrying to them, but doesn't fall into any of the categories above – for instance those who chew food and then spit it out, or those who are afraid of eating in front of others, or those who eat a diet restricted to a very few items. If the way you use food bothers you, then this book is for you.

The book may also be useful for the families and friends of those described above. Many people see that their loved ones struggle horribly with eating appropriately and are concerned for their physical and emotional welfare. If you are in that situation you have probably discovered long since that good advice doesn't seem to help and may even seem to make things worse. You may have discovered that the person you love can't bear to have the subject of food or weight discussed. You probably feel pretty helpless; you want to be of use, but you don't know how. My hope is that this book will give you a way of thinking about disordered eating which will enable you to be useful.

The book may also be useful for front-line professionals who find themselves confronted by patients/clients with disordered eating and who don't know how to help. I'm thinking about dieticians, health visitors, practice nurses, diabetic nurses, school nurses, cardiac rehabilitation professionals, exercise professionals, teachers, social workers and others whose role brings them in contact with people who misuse food. Your instinct may be to refer your patient to specialist services, but you have almost certainly already discovered that unless the patient is very far advanced down the path of a diagnosable eating disorder, there is very little hope of getting specialist help. Indeed, if your patient is very overweight you may well find that there is no help available other than conventional dietary advice or commercial weight loss programmes. I hope that this book will give you a conceptual framework for understanding disordered eating and provide you with many strategies for use with that patient group, with liaison with the patient's general practitioner (GP) as appropriate.

It is clearly not possible to say everything that there is to be said about disordered eating in this one book, so there are a number of issues which you will not find. I don't discuss directly how to alter your food intake – there are many books which describe that in detail. I don't describe or do more than mention the cognitive behavioural techniques for changing your eating behaviour and your thought patterns in relation to food. There are books that focus on these strategies. My concern is to help you make sense of your use of food. Some therapists and researchers think this is not important and that the important thing is to change your behaviour now. I agree that the ultimate aim is change in the present, but for many people I have worked with it has also been important to make sense of their own food use as a preliminary to changing it. If you are such a person, this book is for you.

The first chapter of the book describes in detail how I have come to the conclusions I describe. I also use this chapter to explore some of the more detailed implications of having a history of troubled and troubling experiences. Chapter 2 discusses the whole issue of food and its importance to us. If you would prefer to read from Chapter 3 onwards, describing different situations in which people develop disordered eating, you may want to skip these first two chapters altogether or come back to them later. That is of course, up to you, but in this first chapter are some of the important basic exercises which I hope will help you begin to understand what sorts of experiences in the past may have got you to the point where you have a habit of turning to food (or of turning away from it, if you are more anorexic). You might want to look for those exercises and do some of them, even if you don't want to read the detail around them.

In fact as you go through the whole book I would strongly recommend that you pause and do the exercises where they seem relevant to you. You don't have to write anything down if you don't want to, but they will help you think about how your personal circumstances have contributed to your disordered eating.

Either way, the point of the whole book is not just to get you to understand your behaviour around food better, but to help you work towards ways of needing to manipulate food less and being better able to take care of yourself. As you have probably already found, since you are reading this book, this is not a particularly easy process, especially on your own. You might think about whether you would like to find a buddy who would accompany you on your journey towards a better relationship with food. If you can find someone who is willing to keep you company as you work your way through the book and who is willing to listen to what you say without feeling the need to judge you, or even make things better, the process will probably be easier. There may be a relative or a trusted friend (perhaps someone older if you are still a teenager) or maybe someone in your church or some organisation to which you belong. If you are still at school you may be able to find someone on the pastoral care team who is willing to help. Another possibility is that you find yourself a counsellor who will help you explore the issues raised in this book. These days most schools, colleges and universities have counselling services; many GP surgeries offer at least short-term counselling; otherwise there are many community counselling services that offer low or no cost help. You can find a list of them on the British Association for Counselling & Psychotherapy (BACP) website or in other directories – Chapter 12 on resources will tell you more. (If you are the trusted friend reading this, I suggest you read the book in parallel with the person who has asked you to help, but that you also read 'Guidelines for the Non-professional Helper' in Chapter 12, which may be useful to you in knowing how to respond.)

But back to the people who are the principal readership for this book – those whose eating is disordered. I really want you to feel that you have a right to be upset about your worries about food, weight, shape and size, even if no one has given you an official diagnosis. What is important is that you are uneasy about the way you use food. So, let me explain why I use the expression 'disordered eating'. Eating disorders has come to refer to a rather small group of people whose behaviour meets the requirements of international standards of diagnosis. If you want to know exactly what they are you can read more in Chapter 12.

These diagnoses are used in the UK as ways of rationing help. The problem is that there are many people whose eating has some of these characteristics, but not all. You may, for example be someone who restricts your intake very considerably and avoids any kind of fat as far as you possibly can. You may be eating a very limited range of food. This way of living may cause you a lot of distress and be very annoying and upsetting to the people you live with, especially if you have lost a lot of weight as a result; but if you don't fulfil the weight criteria of the diagnoses, you aren't officially anorexic and you will find it difficult to get specialist help, unless of course you can pay for it privately. Or you may be someone who binges and vomits. You may be very upset about this and worried about what you are doing to yourself. When your friends and family find out, as they will in due course, they will also be very concerned, but again, if you don't conform to the exact descriptions of the diagnoses you won't be classed as having an eating disorder. Perhaps you are someone who often binges and as a result has become very overweight. Very few health professionals will recognise you as having an eating disorder anyway, even if it's there in DSM IV,[1] but it's even less likely that you will get specialist help. If you don't see yourself as bingeing, but maybe consistently overeat, or eat all day long, you don't come into those diagnoses, but that's not to say that you aren't upset and miserable about your eating behaviour. Maybe it's because you find yourself in this situation that you're reading this book in the first place.

But the problem with diagnoses is not just that they are used to ration specialist help; the point of diagnosis in the medical world is that it separates one sort of an illness from another. This is important when different illnesses require very different treatments; if the tightness in your chest is something to do with your heart it will receive very different treatment from tightness in your chest that is the result of huge anxiety. If your terrible headache is the result of migraine it will receive very different treatment from a terrible headache that is the result of bleeding from a blood vessel in your brain. There has been a long debate in the world of mental and emotional problems about whether this medical approach is useful and in the case of eating disorders this debate continues to be very vigorous.

Let me tell you where I stand on these issues. A recent article confirmed what practitioners have suspected for a long time, that people whose eating is disordered don't necessarily stick to one sort of eating disorder. It has been known for a while that about a third of those with bulimia have previously been diagnosable with anorexia. It's also been suspected that lots of people move from anorexia to bulimia to binge eating. Now it has been demonstrated clearly that eating disorders are not fixed and can change. It's also been shown that more than half of those who presented themselves to a large eating disorder clinic in England were not diagnosable with either anorexia or bulimia, but had to be allocated to the category of eating disorders not otherwise specified (EDNOS). The very name of the diagnosis implies a sort of desperation about distinguishing in any meaningful way between different forms of eating disorder. Some theorists think that because of all this we should have more and narrower categories of eating disorder, but others, with whom I agree, think that it's more sensible to see all forms of eating disorder as aspects of the same condition.[2]

Surely it is much more important to understand that you have a very problematic relationship with food than it is to put you in a diagnostic category, especially since the available treatments specific to one or the other condition have limited success. To my mind the question is not 'How exactly do you use food?' but 'What is the meaning of you using food the way you do?' However, it's a good idea for you to know what is recommended as treatment for the various kinds of diagnosed eating disorder. You will find some information on that subject in Chapter 12.

It seems to be true that anorexia and bulimia affect far more women than men, but it's not at all clear that this is true of compulsive eating and binge eating. Certainly the figures for obesity are almost exactly the same for men and women. It's also true that, in the past at least, women have been much more concerned about weight, shape and size. Unfortunately, it looks as though men, and young men particularly, might be beginning to be on the receiving end of the same sorts of pressures about their appearance as women. I have been involved with far more women than men as clients, coming to see me about their eating behaviour, and only about 10 per cent of the people who come to my workshops and lectures are men. I have thought about how to deal with this in this book. Most of the examples I give, although not all, are of females, so the pronoun 'she' is used much more often than 'he', but to give the guys a bit of space and time I've written a chapter specifically on men and disordered eating. However, much of the book applies as much to men as to women; the guys will just have to work a bit harder at finding themselves in the stories that I tell.

Finally, before we really get going with the book, there is one more thing. Some of you might want to look at the research literature that lies behind what I say, or read around the subject a bit more. Some of you might want to be sure that what I say is based on good evidence and not just something I dreamed up all by myself. For these reasons I have included a good number of references to the literature on disordered eating. If you have a connection with a university you can find the publications I mention through their websites; otherwise, enter Google Scholar into your browser and then search that (huge) database. Even if you can't get access to the whole article, you can usually read the abstract/summary, which will give you an idea of what has been said. This literature is constantly growing and evolving, so if you want to know more you can search the database for other material.

Chapter One
Disordered Eating and the Uses of Food

The Problem with Food

Most of us, in our highly developed, post-industrial, western culture are having difficulty in maintaining an appropriate relationship with food. In the UK about 55 per cent of women and 65 per cent of men are overweight or obese. About 25 per cent of both men and women are obese and about 2 per cent of us are what is called morbidly or very obese.[1] Much smaller percentages of people have diagnosed eating disorders. Figures are not very reliable but are probably about 1 per cent of the vulnerable age group 12–25 in young women for anorexia nervosa and perhaps 1.5–2 per cent for bulimia nervosa. The estimate for males with anorexia is generally estimated as 10 per cent of the female prevalence.[2] Many more people, both male and female have an uneasy relationship with food. Research suggests that many obese people binge eat[3] and many, many people have anxieties around food that cause them to eat a restricted diet or to adopt unusual, phobic or obsessional behaviour around food.

How is this to be understood? Are there genetic factors that make it difficult for some of us to manage food appropriately? Disordered eating often feels beyond control, so there have been many attempts to explore whether it may have genetic as opposed to environmental origins. Let's look first at anorexia. Restricted eating, which defines anorexia, but is also common among those who are never diagnosed as anorexic, is very unusual. Most of us find reducing our food intake extremely difficult. We may lose our appetites after an emotional upheaval such as the end of a relationship, or a tremendous shock, such as redundancy, but otherwise bingeing or overeating is more likely to be the problem. Just because restricting food is so unusual a good deal of effort has gone into researching whether it has genetic origins. The tentative answer seems to be 'Well, possibly, it might have.' Twin studies suggest that it is commoner in those with identical genetic inheritance. Work that is probably more useful to understanding and managing anorexia, suggests that people with a specific sort of personality are more vulnerable to it. Personality is probably largely inherited and those with a drive for thinness and obsessionalism may be at greater risk. But we also know that genes can be switched on or off by the environment, so even those with some genetic risk can have that risk increased or decreased by the circumstances, especially of their early lives.[4]

When it comes to overeating, it seems clear that a very large number of us have inherited the capacity to eat a great deal at any one time, to put on weight easily and to lose it with difficulty.[5] These characteristics are now very unhelpful in a society where food is abundant, but for the vast majority of human history the food supply has been uncertain. In the UK it has only been since the 1960s that food has been so inexpensive and abundant that no one in our society need go hungry. It is shocking to realise that as recently as the 19th century large numbers of people in Britain died of starvation.[6] At all times up to the last 50 years the survival of most people would have depended on their capacity to eat large amounts when food was available and to put on weight as a result. Not surprising then that, since we did survive, genetically speaking, many of us have that capacity. Certainly it is common now for people to eat as though they did not know where the next meal was coming from. And with that characteristic, most of us have inherited the tendency to put on weight easily. Most of us know someone who is not like that – someone who can 'eat like a horse and never put on an ounce'. Often such people are tall and thin; I have a private fantasy that they were the ones who were needed to chase down the game in our pre-agrarian history. There are not many of us with this genetic make-up; presumably most people like that did not survive. Ironically, they may be the ones with the best chance of survival now. Most of the rest of us are struggling to lose the weight we put on because we ate too much.

We are not helped in our attempts to form an appropriate relationship with food by the fact that we are dealing with unprecedented abundance of food, available for relatively less than it has ever cost. Where food is scarce, it is precious. In societies where there is food scarcity, survival depends on treating food carefully and using it well. Overweight is then a sign of prosperity and fertility. For us, food has become so cheap and available that we use it for all sorts of purposes – as amusement (think food fights) or art form (think Heston Blumenthal). We waste enormous amounts of it because we insist that it should look perfect – so one third of fruit and vegetable crops is discarded for cosmetic reasons.[7] We throw away a third of what we buy because we buy too much or decide we don't like it or need it.[8] So then food can be used however we choose. One of the uses we have found for it is to soothe and comfort us – we even have the expression 'comfort eating'.

The Emotional Use of Food

So although this book recognises that genetic inheritance and current food abundance make it hard to achieve a calm and reasoned approach to food, its main focus is on the emotional uses that we make of food. In the past 50 years food has become the substance we can all use to help get us through the day, the coping mechanism, the thing that will soothe us or calm us or reward us when life gets too difficult. However, it is also true that, so far as we know, all human societies have used food for emotional purposes. We are familiar with the idea that food is used to mark life events: weddings, funerals, the birth of a child, coming of age. This has gone on for thousands of years. Now that food is so much more abundant we mark almost every social or emotional event with food. Very few meetings between people take place without at least some food and drink, even if it's only tea and biscuits. We also recognise that some situations may result in not eating for some people: anxiety may make it difficult to eat, as may depression or grief. In other words the emotional use of food is normal, and probably always has been, and nearly all of us are using it like that to some extent.[9]

However, when we use food so much that it becomes a problem, then we need to think about what is going on with us. Unfortunately, for very many of us, in the process of using it to help us deal with our emotions, food has also become the enemy. I meet many people who are upset by the way they use food, whether too much or too little. As far as they know, they want to be able to eat without so much anguish; they want food to be ordinary, but it isn't. Often when they talk about themselves they use all sorts of abusive and violent language. They say they are 'just stupid', or 'greedy', or 'have no willpower', or 'can't help themselves', or that they 'hate themselves', 'feel ugly', 'hate thinking about food all the time', 'feel exhausted by their obsessional thinking', 'wish there was no such thing as food'. Above all, they know what they should be doing, what they should be eating, to be healthy and satisfied, 'but just can't do it'.

This book is written for those people because I believe it is possible to understand our eating. When we understand what drives us, then we have choice about what to do. Understanding makes sense of behaviour that makes us feel bad about ourselves and immediately makes us feel better. Sometimes people are so upset by their eating behaviour and their distress about their appearance and their worries about their weight that they can't even bear to acknowledge the problem. This is particularly true of those who are more anorexic. They are very afraid that admitting to the difficulties will mean that they have to give up a way of life that after all has seemed like a solution. But however you use food, you don't do it just by accident; it has a purpose and a meaning and in order to give up misusing food you will have to find other ways of looking after yourself.

Understanding is the first step in developing other ways of managing our lives than by using food. I don't think that any of us are doing things that we think will be bad for us – all of us are trying, often in strange ways, to do the best we can for ourselves. None of us is trying to be unhappy. The person who appears to be starving herself to death is, in my understanding, protecting herself, or using starvation as a way of coping or distracting herself. If she understood better what she was doing, she might be able to find other ways of managing. Similarly, the person who binges and purges, or the person who routinely eats far more than she wants or needs, or the person who gets up in the night to eat, or the person who chews food only to spit it out again, all of them are, I believe, in a strange way, trying to take care of themselves. They are all of them doing the best they can, but their way of managing their lives, of coping, has turned out to be more of a problem than they can handle. What perhaps began as the solution to a problem has become the problem itself, while the original problem remains.

Stop and Think

How would you describe your eating behaviour?
- What are you doing with food?
- Are you restricting your intake?
- Are you bingeing and purging?
- Are you consistently overeating?
- Or is there some other way that you have found to use it – perhaps by only eating one sort of food, or by eating during the night?
- Does it seem possible that you might be trying to achieve something for yourself by your eating behaviour?
- Do you think your eating behaviour might be triggered by thoughts or feelings or events?
- Would you describe yourself as a comfort eater?

Using Food to Manage our Lives

Why do some of us react to life's challenges by using food? And more to the point, how can that be changed? Can it really change? In what follows I want to explain what a huge amount of research has discovered about the way we learn to manage our lives. This research, I believe, provides a way of understanding why some people need to use food. It also provides a clear picture of what needs to change for our food use to be different.

But let's start with the whole concept of managing our lives. Maybe you don't think of yourself as 'managing' your life at all. Maybe it feels to you as if life just happens. But I am sure that each day, every day, we are all deciding how to react to events big and small.

Let's take an example. You have a boyfriend whose name is Paul. You've been with him for nearly three months and you really like him; you think he likes you. He says he thinks you're beautiful and he bought you a silver chain with a heart on it. Since you've been with him you've felt wonderful, everything has seemed easy. You have even been helpful at home and nice to your little sister. But yesterday you heard from one of your friends that he kissed another girl at a party. You didn't really believe her at first, you thought she was just being mean, but then you saw on Facebook that the girl he kissed was boasting about it. You are completely gutted. What are you going to do? Maybe you will find Paul as soon as you can and ask him what he thinks he's doing; you'll be really angry with him and maybe he'll be sorry and you will get back together. But perhaps you are much too upset to talk to him, so you tell your mum and she comforts you. But maybe you don't get on that well with your mum and she doesn't know about Paul anyway because you don't tell her those kinds of things. You would like to talk to your friends about it, but you suspect they will secretly be laughing at you. So what do you do? You say to yourself that if you were thinner Paul would never have betrayed you like that, so you decide that you won't eat today. Maybe you said that to yourself, but you couldn't manage not to eat, so you binged secretly when you were home alone and then threw up. Or maybe you used to make yourself throw up but you don't seem to be able to do that any longer, so you bought all sorts of rubbish to eat and stuffed your face while you were coming home from college, so that you feel disgusting and have to go and lie down in your room when you get home.

And here's another example. You have an appointment to take your car to the garage today. They have asked you to have it there by 10.30 am. However, all sorts of things have delayed you so you're not going to get there before 11.30. There is a wide range of possible ways for you to react. You might simply phone the garage to tell them that you are going to be late, and ask them if that is okay (that would be the calm, grown-up way to do it!). You might say to yourself that it isn't a major problem, these things happen, and you will get there as soon as you can. You might tell yourself that you don't care whether you're late – it's not your problem. But you might instead get very angry with the people and things that have delayed you (the children who didn't get ready for school on time; the traffic that kept you in a queue; the post office that was very slow in serving the customers before you). You might get very anxious about being late, so that you start to feel knots in your stomach, or feel your breathing getting more rapid, or even have the beginnings of a panic attack. Or you might worry about whether the garage people will be annoyed with you or even refuse to take the car in. You might get so upset about being late that you just decide you are going to abandon the whole idea and lie to the garage that you forgot. These sorts of feelings might be so difficult for you to handle that you smoke a cigarette (or two). You might distract yourself from the problem by thinking about something else, for instance, going out that evening, or how many calories you have eaten/will eat that day. You might abolish the problem for a while by making a cup of coffee and eating some biscuits. You might take some chocolate with you in the car and eat it on the way to the garage because you feel so stressed.

These are all possible ways of dealing with a bit of a crisis in your life. You have to manage it because it has happened whether you like it or not. You can probably identify how you would react in a similar situation. If you think about it, you may see that you usually react in the same way to day-to-day problems, and maybe to life's bigger challenges as well. I would call that your typical way of managing your life and I would expect that since you are reading this book your typical way of reacting may very well be something to do with food. Maybe you start to think about how many calories you will eat that day; maybe you plan a binge; maybe you turn to food immediately, long before you have figured out that you are using food to help you. I'm not necessarily suggesting that you are aware of making this choice. Most people who use food like this don't really recognise that they use it in particular ways to deal with particular problems. However, if you start to see that maybe this strategy applies to you then, you are already beginning to create a little thinking space for yourself.

Perhaps it's a new idea that you are managing your life via food – and remember, managing by not eating is just as much a use of food as managing by bingeing and purging, or by continued overeating. If so, it's important that you recognise that even if your disordered eating has caused you enormous problems, you have been trying to do the best for yourself. You have adopted this strategy (almost certainly without consciously knowing that is what you were doing) because it was the best strategy you could find at the time when you started. You can respect yourself for that. You were trying to help yourself.

Stop and Think

Think about the last time that you found yourself eating more than you needed or wanted; or the last time you had a binge; or the last time that you made a resolution to skip a meal or to reduce your food intake. Now think about that day and what happened. What went on that day? What did you have to deal with? Had something happened to upset you or annoy you? Often people who use food are unaware of their feelings to such an extent that they don't really notice how they react to day-to-day events. Spend a little time just considering whether your eating behaviour may have been in response to something that happened.

Since you are reading this book it is likely that you have got to the point of wishing you didn't use food like that any more. That's good. You will need to be dissatisfied with your current strategy for life management in order to learn another. I call it creative discontent. We none of us change easily; change is far too difficult for it just to be something that might be a good idea. We change when we are so fed up with the way things are that we are willing to go through the discomfort of finding another way. What I am hoping to do in this book is help you to understand precisely why you 'took up' food in the first place, so that you will understand the need to manage another way and embark on the journey to find one. Then I hope you will be able to use some of the many ways I describe of finding a better way.

How We Learn to Deal with Life

So let's think about how we learn to deal with life. If you think of a baby, it's clear the baby doesn't deal with life. He or she depends on caregivers to deal with life for them. So the baby needs to be fed and kept clean and clothed by someone else. She needs someone else to soothe her when she's upset or in pain. She needs someone to be able to help her get to sleep and come to her when she wakes. She needs emotional warmth and care and understanding, so that she feels a safe and secure little person. And most babies looked after like this, will be contented and happy (most of the time).[10]

There are two variables in this picture: one is the baby and the other is the caregiver. With rare exceptions, babies come ready, willing and able to relate to their caregivers. You only need to approach a baby to see that she is trying to make contact with you through her eyes, through turning her head to watch you, through the noises that she makes, through the conversations that she conducts by kicking her legs. But babies undoubtedly come with different temperaments and personalities; they also come with different physical constitutions. If a baby is unwell or has some sort of disability or delayed development, she will be more likely to suffer discomfort and less likely to respond easily to her caregivers. So, in a common example, babies come with an immature digestive system, so tend to suffer in the early months from what we as adults would call indigestion, which in babies is called colic. This makes them uncomfortable so they cry – crying being the only means open to them of expressing distress. In the same way babies cry when they are teething, because obviously it hurts to have those sharp little bits of bone pushing through their gums. More significant physical ailments will create more significant and lasting distress.

But difference in personality also creates difference in how babies respond to their caregivers. Some can be soothed more easily than others. Some babies are more sensitive than others, react to noise more strongly, are more apt to cry or to find it difficult to relax and sleep. Some babies need more sleep than others; some babies are more active than others; some babies seem to need more holding than others, and so on. Inherited characteristics become more obvious as we get older – 'he's good at maths like his father'; 'she has a real talent for singing, my family are all like that'; 'she's really outgoing like her mother'; 'she's desperately shy, I was like that growing up but her sister is much more confident' – but they are there from the beginning. How important these innate characteristics will turn out to be, for better or worse, depends largely on the child's experience growing up.

Stop and Think

- What have you heard about your constitutional and genetic inheritance?
- Have you heard stories about what sort of a baby you were?
- Have you physical characteristics or talents like someone else?
- Who do you get compared to in your family?
- Who do you think has a temperament like yours?
- Who do you feel is most like you?
- Does that help you understand more about yourself?

The other variable is the caregiver. Unfortunately, the baby has no choice about who her caregivers are or how capable they are of looking after her. They in turn have been influenced by whatever their early experience was like. If your mother was lucky enough to be loved and well taken care of as a child, chances are she will be able to do the same for you – or not.

Whatever the baby's personality or physical condition, she depends very heavily on her caregivers to manage her life so that she experiences as little discomfort, pain or frustration as possible. This is of course an almost impossible task. Every baby's (person's) life is full of minor distress – feeling cold or lonely or in pain or frightened, for example. Even the best and most competent mother will find it impossible to iron out every upset. (I am going to use 'mother' as the general word for the main caregiver, but of course that role is not only taken on by mothers. Some fathers are the main caregivers; often grandmothers have an important role; some children are brought up by their sisters or fostered or adopted. There are many different possibilities. It is important to recognise that babies need one or very few main caregivers, but that role can be taken by all sorts of people. Mother is just a convenient shorthand for the one who took that role in your life.)

Stop and Think

- Who was your main caregiver when you were a baby and a child, as early as you know or can remember?
- Was there more than one?
- Which three words would you now use to describe the memory you have of that person/those people at that time in your life?
- How good do you think she or he was at taking care of you?

Just because it is impossible to protect the baby/small child/ bigger child from every stone on life's path, it's important that the mother teaches the child how to deal with upsets by herself. What seems to happen is that the baby/small child learns to talk to herself and others in the way the mother talks to her. I remember, for instance, a child of about six who was rather a daydreamer and was often told, with varying degrees of exasperation, 'Just, get on with it, Alice!' So when she was playing cricket with her family and her grandfather took a long time to bowl, she shouted, 'Just get on with it, Grandpa!' It is highly likely that she talked to herself in that way too, in a rather impatient and irritated way. It seems that we learn to talk to others and to ourselves in just the way we have been talked to.

> "Research has shown that the way we relate to *ourselves* – whether we regard ourselves kindly or critically, in a friendly and affectionate way or hostilely – can have a major influence on our ability to get through life's difficulties and create within ourselves a sense of well-being."
> —Gilbert, *The Compassionate Mind*, 2009[11]

In a good situation the majority of those interactions with main caregivers will be positive when things go wrong. In early life that positive response will mostly be conveyed by hugging and holding, probably accompanied by soothing words. As a child gets older a positive response will also be conveyed with soothing, understanding and reassuring words such as 'It's all right'; 'Never mind, we'll fix it'; 'What a pity you forgot, let's see what we can do about it'; Oh, you must have been very upset, poor you'; 'What a horrid thing to happen; you must have been very angry'; 'Oh, you really hurt your knee, let's kiss it better and put a big plaster on it'. If we had that kind of response as children we can probably do the same for ourselves now and say to ourselves, when bad things happen, 'It's all right. I can handle this. It's a pity and I wish it hadn't happened, but it will be okay.'

Stop and Think

– What memories do you have of how you were responded to when things went wrong when you were young?

– What sorts of things can you remember being said to you when (for instance) you lost something or forgot something, or made a mistake, or broke something, or hurt yourself?

– On the basis of this evidence, how well do you think your main caregiver was capable of supporting you in difficult situations?

Caregivers Who Don't Do It Very Well

Huge amounts of research have demonstrated that the child who has caregivers capable of responding accurately to the child's mood will grow up much more confident and secure than children whose caregivers do not respond so well.[12] You can see failings of this kind on any high street or in any supermarket. I was idly gazing out of my office window one day when I saw a mother and child walking along the street. The child was about nine years old and wanted to hold her mother's hand. The mother refused to hold the child's hand and ended up walking along the street with her hand in the air while the child held on to her skirt. Whatever that child's need at that moment, the mother could not or would not respond to it. Another day I was in a shopping mall and saw a child of about four with several people including the father. The child was tired and complaining so after a number of impatient responses the father smacked the child. It is not a pretty sight to see a grown man smack a small child – clearly he was incapable of dealing with the child in a more understanding (and adult) way. There are of course many more gross examples of failure of care; roughly two children die each week in the UK at the hands of those who are supposed to look after them. Roughly two thirds of us have caregivers who give us what we need; a third of us don't.

The lapses and inadequacies of caregivers are by no means always deliberate or ill-intentioned. Many parents find themselves in situations that reduce their capacity to pay as much attention to a baby or child as that small person needs. There can be circumstances such as unavoidable separations (perhaps the caregiver's illness, mental or physical, or worse still death); the illness or disability or death of another family member; difficulties in the parents' relationship; the breakdown of the parents' relationship; the arrival of a step-parent/step-sibling; difficult financial circumstances; the demands of earning a living. Where anyone in the family has an addiction or obsessive or compulsive illness (including eating disorders), the care and attention given to other members of the family will almost certainly be badly affected.

But even when day-to-day circumstances are relatively all right, many parents have themselves had experience as children of neglect or abuse; these experiences will impact on their capacity to parent their own children better. Although some parents with a history of abuse or neglect bravely and actively make it their business to overcome their own disadvantages and do better for their children, many do not.

No caregivers are perfect and it probably wouldn't be good if they were. We all need to be able to develop a bit of resilience by ourselves in difficult situations; but we will learn to manage our lives with compassion and understanding for ourselves if that is what we have experienced when we were young. The opposite also seems to be true. As babies and children we have no way of contextualising the responses that come our way. If we are generally seen as lovable and enjoyable, we will very likely grow up with that image of ourselves. Conversely, if we are seen as 'naughty', 'bad', 'horrible', 'evil', 'just winding me up', 'deliberately being annoying', that message will also go deep and last a lifetime. I remember once being in a supermarket and seeing a mother berating a child of about four for knocking something off a shelf. She spoke to the child so violently that I tried to intervene and say that it had been an accident. The mother turned on me and spat out, 'It wasn't an accident; he's a horrible little boy.' The look on the child's face was heartbreaking; he had no defences against that attack, no way of saying to himself that his mother was unfair and that what she said was untrue; or even supposing it had been true, of recognising that her behaviour was a gross overreaction. When life gets difficult for that child when he gets older, how will he be able to soothe and reassure himself and find a calm and rational response to his mistakes? And how will he be able to believe that other people will support and help him when things are difficult if his experience has been that when he makes a mistake other people turn on him and attack him?

There are also quite a lot of parents who want their child(ren) to fulfil some purpose for them. We have heard about tennis fathers and ballet mothers – parents whose overwhelming need has been for the child to accomplish something for them. Some parents want their child 'to be a credit to them', which usually means that the child should look the right way, dress the right way, behave the right way in public, pass the right exams, know the right people, go to the right university. It is very difficult for a child born into this situation to find her own way of being; having an eating disorder can be a means of separating from parents who glue their children to them. It can be a means of translating into eating behaviour those feelings of resistance and rebellion that are too difficult to allow into consciousness.

When young women are lonely and miserable they can imagine that a baby will be the one to make them feel loved and valued, so that child can grow up feeling that its role in life is to look after the mother. How will that child learn to take care of her own needs appropriately? How much of a temptation will it be to meet her own emotional needs by the use of a substance – alcohol, drugs, or maybe food? Or will she repeat the cycle of having a child very young in the hope of being loved?

These ideas about the importance of how our caregivers looked after us have been very extensively researched over the past 50 years and are no longer in doubt. They are known as the theory of attachment – 'attachment' being the word used to describe the relationship between the child and the caregiver.

Stop and Think

What message did you get from your caregivers about you and what they wanted you to be? Was it, for instance, 'Be successful', 'Be clever', 'Be perfect', 'Look after me', 'Don't cause me any trouble', 'Don't make a fuss'. 'Don't leave me', 'Always be happy', 'You're not important', 'Other people are more important than you', 'I don't care what you feel', 'It's time you stood on your own two feet'?

In the past 20 years or so it has become clear that there is a connection between difficult beginnings and disordered eating.[13] It seems clear that many people who are preoccupied with what they eat or don't eat are using food as a way of distracting or protecting themselves or coping with or managing memories, thoughts, experiences or feelings that they don't know how to deal with in any other way.

The Consequences of a History of Poor Attachment

What is now known about child development, as a result of the work of neuroscientists, is that growing up without adequate or appropriate support from our caregivers does not just leave us with a gap in our learning (although it does have that effect). It seems to affect the development of our brains. In particular we may not be able to produce those soothing and calming chemicals, such as oxytocin, which help us deal with difficult situations. We will then be very much more likely to find other substances or activities to help us manage in difficult situations (food, alcohol, drugs, self-harm, violence). This way of managing need not be a life sentence; Schore, one of the most interesting of the neuroscientists who have explored this issue, believes that our brains can change and that we can learn to do things differently, can learn to soothe ourselves and develop trusting relationships with others.[14] But nobody is saying that is an easy process.

The fundamental problem is that if we have not been appropriately soothed and have not had carers who have sufficiently helped us to manage our feelings, we are likely to have great difficulty managing them as we grow up and in adult life.[15] We badly need the skills of emotional regulation because otherwise we are at the mercy of our feelings. Everyone knows people who can't manage their anger and who explode with rage, often creating huge problems in their own lives and those of others. These people have never learned to deal with angry feelings. We probably know others who never say what is going on with them, but always pretend that everything is fine. Many people, of whom you may be one, self-soothe not with words and compassion but with substances and activities. The compulsive exerciser is making himself feel better by his exertion; the drug addict or problem drinker is using substances to escape from feelings he can't manage; the person with disordered eating is using her preoccupation with food, weight, shape and size to deal with feelings that she doesn't know how to manage in any other way.

So far what I have been emphasising is that a history of good attachment will give you the huge advantage of being able to soothe yourself and enable you to trust other people. These are what I call the gold standard strategies for getting you through life. I'm suggesting that if your beginnings haven't been all that good (not necessarily terrible and not necessarily because someone is to blame) you will find it difficult to use these gold standard strategies and will have to develop other ways of coping. These may include using food. Let's try and unpick a bit further the problems created by difficult beginnings.

Difficulty in Forming Mature, Mutually Intimate Relationships

Many people have commented on the way that difficulties with attachment make it hard for us to form good relationships later on in life. It seems that 75 per cent of us will stick with the same sort of relationships which we have experienced in our families of origin, for better or for worse. The template of what a relationship is like seems to be very enduring, even if at a conscious level we haven't liked or enjoyed the original experience. That helps to explain why we tend to choose the same kinds of partner; some women get rid of one violent or alcoholic man, only to choose another just the same, while others replace one highly organised, controlling partner with another. Of course it's a fine system if our original experience has been good. I have watched how young women from kind, concerned, nurturing backgrounds have found men who will be loving husbands and good fathers. It's easier to choose well if you know what to choose. The trouble is that if we repeat our experience and choose badly, we continue that same situation of having no one to trust and no one to support us. In that context having food as your best friend starts to make a lot of sense.[16]

Stop and Think

Think back to the exercise above where you tried to describe the kind of relationships you had with your main caregivers. Do you think you have repeated those patterns in the intimate relationships you have developed since? How would you feel about consciously and actively choosing your partner using a tick list of qualities? Could you learn to love someone very different from your early relationship experience, if that was not good?

Lack of Body Awareness

In a good situation we develop an awareness of our bodies and of physical sensations quite early in our development. So, for instance, we will recognise feelings of cold or tiredness, hunger or pain – or rather, we will be taught to recognise those feelings by those looking after us. Attentive parents will be aware that hungry children become bad tempered and irritable, so they will plan ahead to ensure that their child is fed appropriately and on time. One mother I knew used to carry a cheese sandwich in her bag for her little boy so that when she noticed the signs of hunger she would say to him, 'Paul, I think you're hungry. Come and get this sandwich.' We can expect that as he grows up Paul will know what hunger feels like and make sure he eats. Concerned caregivers will also look after a child who is hurt; good mothers kiss hurt knees better and use big plasters to help with the fright and pain of falling down. But if your mother thought it was sissy to make a fuss about falling down or told you it didn't hurt, then you will learn not to notice when you hurt yourself, and maybe even find it possible to hurt yourself without feeling anything much. Good caregivers will also

Stop and Think

- How aware do you think you are of your physical sensations and responses?
- Do you know when you are hungry/tired/sad/angry/ anxious etc?
- Could you describe what those feelings feel like in your body?
- Are you the sort of person who finds a bruise on your leg and doesn't remember how it got there?
- What kind of an education do you think you had in body awareness in your family of origin?
- Who was concerned for your physical and emotional welfare?

help you be aware of physical feelings that signal emotions – they will notice when you are lethargic because of sadness or agitated because of anxiety. Many people who use food to manage don't really know what they feel and are dissociated from their physical sensations. Since we know what we feel emotionally because of physical signals, this makes reacting appropriately very difficult.[17] If you don't know what it is that you feel, it can sometimes be a relief to respond to yourself with food or you may easily mistake other feelings, especially anxiety, for hunger.

Lack of an Emotional Language

On these foundations of body awareness can be built an emotional language. Again, we are largely dependent on our caregivers to teach us that language. There is a good deal of research that shows that people with disordered eating of all kinds find it hard to connect words and feelings.[18] This doesn't mean that you don't know words such as 'sad', 'disappointed', 'jealous', etc. It just means that you don't connect those words with your own physical feelings and your own experience. Lots of people with disordered eating are aware of some feelings, but others remain out of awareness.

Stop and Think

 Try a little test. Time yourself for one minute and see how many feeling words you can write down in that time. If you score 15 or more you clearly don't have any problem with an emotional vocabulary, but if you can only think of 5 or 6 it may be that you are not used to describing your experience in terms of feelings. Does that sound like you?

It is very difficult to describe your own history and experience if you haven't enough words to do it with. This lack of means of expression can result in you using something other than words to indicate what is going on with you – maybe bingeing or starving, rather than talking. The problem with these strategies is that they indicate something is wrong, but they say nothing about what is wrong. They make it difficult for other people to help because the language of food and the body is so imprecise.

Lack of Self-nurture

As we grow up we are constantly being taught whether we should see ourselves as valuable and important or whether we are not worth bothering about. I had a friend who used to tell the story of how her mother would watch her getting ready to go out as a teenager and sneer, 'Who do you think is looking at you?' It's hard to take good care of yourself and think you are worth taking care of if you have had that message drummed into you. It is also interesting that a brand of cosmetics has for some time now used the slogan 'Because you're worth it' as a way of getting women to buy their products. It suggests that many of us have difficulty in feeling that we are worth taking care of. If your early experience is of neglect – that nobody cares about you – then you will almost certainly find it very difficult to care about yourself. With this kind of mindset it is difficult to ensure that you eat well and regularly, that you take good care of yourself physically, that you ensure that you are warm enough, rested enough, active enough. I had one anorexic client who used to walk everywhere, whatever the weather, rather than using public transport. Part of her motivation was to lose weight, but in the process she ignored the exhaustion she felt, so that she came to see me with huge black smudges of fatigue under her eyes. I have also had many clients who were very big, who scarcely moved all day long. Part of their difficulty is that they are too heavy to feel comfortable being active, but in the process they ignore their fundamental need to move their bodies and as a result have many aches and pains. One of the rewards of the work that I do is to see women who start attending groups with un-washed hair and the most basic of clothes – tracksuit bottoms and a T-shirt – gradually starting to take care of themselves and, whatever their size, showing signs of believing that they might be worth looking after.

Stop and Think

How would you score yourself out of 10 on self-nurture, where 10 means 'I take good care of myself' and 0 means 'I find it almost impossible to believe that I'm worth bothering with'? If you score 6 or less, can you identify how you have learned to think so little of yourself? Who or what has taught you that you aren't worth taking care of?

Lack of Self-esteem

Difficulty in taking care of yourself, in the way I describe above, is one aspect of self-esteem. Self-esteem is our way of evaluating ourselves and can vary over different parts of our lives. Often people whose eating is disordered can hold down a job perfectly well but may find relationships very difficult or are full of loathing for the way they look. As children our self-esteem is mostly derived from our interactions with our parents; they are the ones who can make us feel that we are loved and enjoyable people. As we get older we rely increasingly on our other experiences to tell us about ourselves. Teenage girls in particular are intensely critical and can conduct vicious attacks on each other. These attacks, a form of bullying, can destroy a young person's sense of their own value. If your family haven't given you much of a feeling of your own value, that sort of experience in adolescence can be utterly devastating, especially when it is so often coupled with comments about your appearance. One young woman with anorexia that I knew had come from a family where her mother was kind and helpful but overworked. Her father was very critical, however, and as a result she was not particularly confident. When she went to the senior school she found herself the target of a group of three girls who baited and bullied her unmercifully. A lot of their abuse had to do with the way she looked. Her anorexia dated from that time; it was her way of dealing with a situation that she could find no other way to manage.

Lack of a Sense of Self

Just as we depend on our caregivers to teach us about feelings and how to look after ourselves, so we depend on them to help us develop a sense of self, of identity, of who we are. Ideally, we need them to notice who we are and tell us about ourselves in the most positive and creative way they can manage. So we need them to notice what we can do – from pleasure in the small child's tower of bricks to satisfaction in the bigger child's mastery of reading and writing; to acknowledgement of the yet bigger child's accomplishments in sport or music or schoolwork; to interest in and acceptance of the teenager's wish to be different from us, to make their own distinctive mark. The parent's job is to be the mirror for the child in which he can see himself with as little distortion as possible.

This need for mirroring doesn't end with growing up. We all need a continuing source of it throughout our lives. That is why ceremonies that recognise achievement are so important and why most of us are hungry for praise and recognition. Without feedback and response we have great difficulty in knowing who we are. And when you don't know who you are it can be so challenging just to survive. This is when self-soothing with food or preoccupying yourself with how many calories you have eaten may seem an attractive diversion.

Stop and Think

Have a go at checking out your sense of your own value and identity:

Make a list of ten adjectives to describe yourself. You are not allowed to use negative adjectives. If you have difficulty doing this, try thinking how the person who loves you most would describe you. Then look at that list. How would it be if you could acknowledge that those words describe you? Would it make you feel differently about yourself? Would it make life seem easier?

To summarise then, those of us fortunate to have had good early experience will have developed a capacity to self-soothe when things get difficult and will have had the experience which will enable us to choose trustworthy others as friends and partners to help us live our lives supported by them. Our early experience will have enabled us to be aware of our physical selves and so aware of sensations that will lead us to take care of ourselves appropriately – feelings such as hunger, tiredness and pain. This physical awareness will also have extended to those syndromes of sensations which we will have been taught to identify as emotional responses, such as anger, sadness, disappointment, excitement, delight, and so on. Our capacity to have names for these sensations will have enabled us to talk about our day-to-day experience and thus to reflect on it, with caregivers who have demonstrated their interest in and concern for our daily welfare. In turn this interchange, reliably repeated over the years of our growing up, will have provided us with the template for talking to ourselves in a supportive and useful way and given us a clear sense of identity which will gradually consolidate through childhood and adolescence. Together these experiences and capacities will have created strategies for life management that will collectively enable us to deal with life circumstances in a relatively calm and rational way.

The one third of us who are not so fortunate will to varying degrees be struggling with the lack of an appropriate early emotional education. We may well be unaware of physical sensations or capable of numbing ourselves to them, which will make us less able to take good care of ourselves, so that we may find it difficult to give ourselves adequate rest or to feed ourselves appropriately. We may also be able to deaden ourselves to pain, so that we are capable of self-harm. We may be unaware of what it is we feel, or capable of distinguishing only a few emotions, typically anger or sadness. We will almost certainly lack an emotional vocabulary with which to describe our experience and so will remain victims of it, without the capacity to think about it and draw conclusions from it about how to live our lives less painfully. Most of all we will lack the capacity to self-soothe by talking to ourselves in a reassuring and supportive way. Our internal conversation will tend to be full of blame and judgement of ourselves. Finally, we will lack the belief that other people can be useful and helpful and so we will tend to be isolated, or to have contacts with other people that are limited to superficial issues. Very often we may feel that we are putting on a front and that nobody really knows who we are. That real self, we will probably feel, is unattractive to others as well as shameful to ourselves, and to be kept hidden as much as possible.

Living with these limitations makes life very hard. Life is full of day-to-day problems and difficulties for the vast majority of us. Things like managing our money, organising our lives, making friends, finding work that we like and are good at, taking care of our physical needs and so on present us all with dilemmas and challenges on a daily basis. In addition, most of us have to deal with more major life events from time to time: the significant illness or death of someone important to us; the experience of failure in something that we mind about; real anxieties about finance; serious disruption in our lives caused by the ending of a relationship; major challenges due to big changes in our circumstances, including those caused by transition from one life circumstance to another such as moving school, moving house, leaving home, going to college/university, getting married, having children, getting divorced, etc. If we lack the resources described above, especially those of self-soothing and reliance on trusted others, we will really struggle. And that's when we are likely to turn to food.

I mentioned earlier that food is inexpensive and available in our culture, so that makes it a possible substance to use for self-soothing. As we shall see in the next chapter, we all have a lifetime of experience of the soothing power of eating. However, it looks as though eating large amounts – bingeing – may be a particularly effective form of self-soothing because it has specific effects on brain chemistry which make us feel good.[19] In other words, when we use food we are self-medicating,[20] trying to take care of ourselves. And of course such behaviour is likely to be repeated.

And so…

At this point it's time for you to think about whether this account of disordered eating makes sense to you. Maybe the following questions will be useful in helping you to think it through.

If you are answering yes to a good number of these questions, then I think that this book may be useful to you. So let me tell you about the rest of the book and how you might use it. The next chapter (2) discusses why food is so very important to all of us and suggests the kinds of experiences that might have made it particularly important to you. Then there are seven chapters that discuss the sorts of experience in your growing up which might have brought you to turn to food as a way of trying to make life better for yourself. Then there is a chapter on body esteem and disordered eating (10) and finally one on disordered eating in men (11). Not all of them will be relevant to you – you will have to look for the situation that most fits your circumstances. It may be that none of the scenarios I describe quite fits you, but I think there will be bits here and there which you can put together to make sense of your own responses to your history.

What I'm hoping is that you will get to the point where your own eating behaviour begins to make sense to you, when you can recognise what you were trying to do by your use of food. But that's just the first step. What I am also trying to help you with is developing another way of coping with life. If that was easy you would have done it long since – it will

Stop and Think

1. Does it seem likely to you that your times of disordered eating or your worries about shape, weight and size are triggered by specific thoughts, memories, events or feelings?
2. Do you tell yourself off and criticise yourself when things go wrong?
3. Do you find it difficult to talk about what bothers you to other people? Do you tend to keep your worries and upsets to yourself? Do you edit what you tell other people about yourself so that they don't really know when things are not going well for you?
4. Do you sometimes find it hard to know what you are feeling or find it hard to put it into words?
5. When you think about your growing up, does it seem true to you that not enough attention (for whatever reason) was paid to what was going on with you and what you felt and thought?
6. Are there times in your past that you find it too painful to think about?
7. Do you sometimes feel that you don't know what you want or who you are?
8. Do you find it hard to bother about looking after yourself?
9. Does it seem at all likely to you that your disordered eating is your way of coping with life and that's why it's so hard to give it up?

take time and effort. Do the exercises that seem most relevant to you and practise making the changes that seem most likely to help you. You may very well feel that you could use more help, once you start to realise how you can understand your eating behaviour. In that case the resources in Chapter 12 should be helpful to you. In reading this book you are having the courage to start on a journey towards self-knowledge and the capacity to reflect on your life.

One more thing – you may think that everything that I have said so far is a roundabout way of blaming your parents and caregivers for the way they brought you up. Some, very few, parents are actively cruel and hostile to their children; most are doing the best they can, even when that best isn't very good. All of them have been influenced deeply by what happened to them as they grew up, just as you have been. What I am trying to do is not to blame them (because that doesn't help) but get you to think about just what those influences have been and how they have affected you. Of course you will have feelings about those influences; you may be very angry with your parents and caregivers; you may hate them. But just at the moment that is irrelevant to your problems with food. The difficulties of your beginnings may very well have led to you choosing food to manage your life. Now the issue is how you can choose another way.

Chapter Two
Thinking About Food

"Sundays we always used to go to my grandmother's and she always bought the most enormous chicken you could buy without being a turkey and you were allowed to gorge yourself on everything. And she would bake two apple pies for afters, because she knew we were all pigs. And that was about two o'clock, and by four o'clock she'd already made the scones; we had a cream tea. That's what we did every Sunday unless she was ill, and then my mother did it."

— Research participant

"My mum is a fantastic cook . . . and as a child I can just always remember that our house was always filled with people either staying, or visiting. …She used to cook all the time. My father was a clergyman so … they entertained a lot through that. There was always things going on at church and she'd be baking all the time. So … food was quite a major thing I guess in our house."

— Research participant

Although I have stressed the fact that eating disorders are not just about food and that I am concerned to explore what lies behind them, yet it is important to pay some attention to why we might choose this way of expressing our inner selves. For each of us food and eating have a long history and a lifetime of meaning. We can probably begin to find some clues about why we use food in the way we do in the story of our experience of it. In this chapter I want to trace some of our memories of and associations to food during the course of our development. Your part in this process is to recreate your own history and see if you can glimpse some of the inner logic behind your use of food now.

Early Experiences of Food

Good feeding experiences as babies are important because they leave us with memory traces of blissful states which we may later try to recapture. We come into the world totally dependent on our caregivers for our life to continue, but the vast majority of us are ready to play our part by being able and willing to suck. The baby is hungry, the food appears, the baby sucks and is satisfied. The image of a satisfied, contented baby going off to sleep in its mother's arms is a powerful symbol of total happiness, total security.

However, for many the early experiences of food, of hunger, of eating, are not always straightforward. It takes confidence to feed a tiny baby well and in our western culture mothers are often not very confident. We do not always match the baby's need for food soon enough, quickly enough, accurately enough to prevent distress. It is now half a century since it was recognised by psychologically aware paediatricians, such as Donald Winnicott,[1] what agony that sense of acute hunger arouses in the baby. Hunger is something the infant cannot name, cannot understand or account for, but only suffer. As adults most of us have experienced hunger immediate enough to cause pain, maybe even panic, but we have a whole world of understanding into which to fit those feelings

and with which to help us cope with them. The baby has no
such containing framework.

Very few of us can consciously remember those early feeding
experiences. We want to believe that they have no effect on
us, but it seems very likely that the intensity of that feeding
experience remains with us in some preconscious, non-verbal
way. For those who misuse food, these earliest experiences may
well be one element in later difficulties. Charlene had been
among those babies who actually experienced starvation. Her
mother was simply not equal to the fierce demands of looking
after a baby. Charlene was kept alive with ice lollies until at
six months old she was taken from her mother and put into
care. As a young adult Charlene became a compulsive eater
who was never full enough, never satisfied.

Of course, that is not the whole story. A baby's experience
of being fed is also the experience of being loved, held, taken
care of, protected. Missing out on one of these experiences
means missing out on the others as well. Charlene's compulsive
eating was not only an endless attempt to undo the real
physical neglect of 20 years earlier, but also an attempt to
repair the emotional hurt and damage. It is easy to see in this
case how hopeless an enterprise that was; perhaps Charlene's
hurts could be healed by better experience of being loved,
but certainly they could not be healed by compulsive eating.

For some of us of a certain generation, there was the
difficulty that our mothers were taught to disregard their
natural urges to pick us up and feed us when we cried and
were hungry. Truby King was the male author of manuals on
infant care who urged mothers to believe that it was actually
harmful for babies to be fed at other than strict four-hourly
intervals, however much they cried, and that babies should
not be handled more than was strictly necessary.[2] A modern

version of this style of parenting has been advocated by Gina Ford and has aroused passionate and even violent discussion.[3] The suffering of a sensitive mother who feels pressurised by these theories is surely equal only to the suffering of the baby who receives such treatment – how many adults eat only at four-hourly intervals, never mind babies. These babies must have had the most terrible early physical and emotional experience of the pangs of hunger.

Another major event in our infant experience of feeding is weaning. Very few mothers have the freedom — practical or emotional — and the confidence to wait and see what their baby wants and needs and when it will happily, and with curiosity and pleasure, begin to explore the interesting possibilities of mixed feeding. For many babies the weaning process may feel like something frightening and depriving; something known and good is being taken away and replaced by something strange and difficult and unpleasant. The sweet milk (and it is remarkable just how sweet breast milk is; cows' milk has sugar added to it as part of the process of modifying it for babies) is replaced by an alien texture and taste.

It seems likely that these early feeding experiences can underlie various sorts of food misuse. One is the feeling of not being able to rely on there being food again — the need to eat to satiety now because the opportunity will not come again. An echo of weaning perhaps lies in the preference of many food misusers for foods that are sweet and easy to eat, requiring little chewing. Could this be why fast food chains are so successful and why so many people like ice cream and soft drinks? Maybe a lot of us learned to doubt and misunderstand our feelings of hunger. Probably most of us did not have enough of that early experience of breast/bottle feeding so we find culturally approved ways of making up to ourselves for the nasty shock of it being brought to an end so soon. I am interested, for instance, in how water is now sold in half-litre bottles that have what can only be described as a teat on the end, so that the water is extracted by sucking. It is fascinating to see people using a feeding bottle without apparently any recognition that they are doing so.

There is a great deal more to eating disorders than the attempt to reverse or recreate early feeding experience, but the central importance of that experience in our infant lives makes it worth considering and investigating.

Stop and Think

If you want to think about your misuse of food it might be worth trying to explore that subject by talking to those who knew you as a baby. You could ask what they remember about how you were fed and what kind of a baby you were. Perhaps you can learn something about the roots of your present difficulties in that early history.

Food as Part of an Early Power Struggle

The meaning of food and eating does not derive only from our infant experience. We also have a lifetime of personal meanings to add to those beginnings. The next in chronological order, and one that may well be within reach of conscious memory for some of us, is the battle that is often conducted over food with toddlers and young children. It is difficult, and probably impossible, to get right the balance between allowing children freedom to choose and appropriately limiting their choices, especially as the territory is always moving anyway. It is easy to offer a 2-year-old the choice between milk and juice, but what about the 8-year-old who wants coffee or the 12-year-old who wants beer?

Unfortunately, food is often chosen as the battleground on which the child's struggle for separation and independence is worked out. These issues are complicated by the meanings of food and feeding as loving and caring that were referred to in connection with infant feeding. Parents, especially mothers, can have too much invested in getting their child to eat up everything. Not eating can too easily be seen as rejection of what has been offered and therefore of the one who offers it. I remember reading advice to mothers not to take too much time or trouble over preparing darling little meals for tiny children. If the child spits out what you have taken hours to make, you are much more likely to be upset than if it took you ten minutes and/or (perish the thought) you opened a packet or a tin.

In this sense of rejection lie the roots of the anger and the power struggle that so frequently follows a child's refusal of food. We know, because we have read it many times, that if a child is normal in every other way and full of energy, then however little food she gets it is enough. This truth can be hard to hang on to when all your child will eat is peanut butter sandwiches, but it is sometimes reassuring. Despite this we nevertheless try and force children to eat. Why? Perhaps it has something to do with the unpalatable fact that as parents it is our function to become unnecessary. In the first intimation of the fact that our child is capable of not wanting what we want is the distant trumpet call that sounds the end of our usefulness in that role. Our violence in reinforcing our will is the measure of how hard it is for us to endure that hard fact.

Gordon and Hilda, a husband and wife both in their fifties, were discussing their experiences with food as children. Hilda told how as a child she was required to eat everything put in front of her, whether she liked it or not and whether she was hungry or not. If she would not eat it she was given nothing else and at each meal what she had previously not eaten was put in front of her until she did. Such brutal and humiliating ways of dealing with children are perhaps not quite as common these days. Gordon then told how he was allowed to eat what he wanted. At one time he ate nothing but bananas and orange juice. At this point in the story Hilda interrupted to say how very spoiled and indulged he had been as a child. The interesting thing is that one of these adults is now what is called a 'picky eater' and dislikes a great many foods. The other is a curious and adventurous eater and will try anything. I will leave you to work out which is which.

Once the power struggle is located in food, then both parties are likely to play the game with great enthusiasm and persistence. That is bad enough in itself, but there is worse to follow. It seems that often the struggle we carried on in reality as small children with our parents, we continue as grown people in our heads. We install the parent figure inside us. We internalise her (him, them) and we continue to respond to this internal parent as we responded, or wanted to respond, to the real parent.

Isobel came from a family where food was in short supply. This was not because there was any lack of money but because Isobel's mother believed in strictly limiting portions of food. She always bought the absolute minimum quantities of everything and never kept any supplies in the cupboard. Each day's food was bought a day at a time and there were no extras to allow for unexpected changes or snacks. So there were never any biscuits or 'instant food' for peckish moments.

Isobel had coped with this mean and depriving household as best she could — because what went with it was a mother who felt that her emotional resources were in as short supply as the food and who found it impossible to respond with generosity to the emotional hunger of her family. As a child Isobel found substitute mothers in her teachers and the families of her friends and then from her mid-teens in sexual relationships with boys considerably older than herself from whom she could get some 'mothering'. This system broke down when she left her home town to go to college. There she began to eat voraciously, eating to fill the void of unlovedness, but also to defy the mother who practised such rigid portion control. To eat a whole packet of biscuits became an act of hatred and revenge against the mother who was now unable to limit Isobel's consumption.

Women and Food – the Dilemma

This account of Isobel and her mother makes clear another aspect of food use that is particularly difficult for women. Mothers (girlfriends, wives, sisters, grannies) are often not only the ones who do the preparing of food, shopping and cooking, but are also the ones required to limit their food intake. Feminists have made us aware of the cultural requirement for women to be thin. As they have pointed out, virtually all women's magazines contain sections on food restriction for women ('The Three Day Diet'; 'Get Your Body Ready for the Beach', etc.). Side by side with these instructions will be others urging them to feed their families ('Hearty Puddings for Your Family'; 'Scrumptious Casseroles for Hungry Men', etc.). The apparent requirement is that we starve ourselves while urging others to eat ('Go on, eat it up, it'll do you good').[4]

This complex message about how to deal with food in relation to our families is paralleled by what is often understood by women as the demand to take care of everyone else and not to take care of themselves. Women are to be generous with others emotionally, take care of their needs and wants, but ignore their own needs. These cultural messages make it extremely hard for women to know whether they are allowed to eat, or certainly what and how much. Many of the women I have talked to say they have an index in their heads of forbidden foods — forbidden, that is, to them but not to others. Food is made to do the work of all kinds of complicated feelings about loving and not loving.

The Role of Food in the Family

This brings us to another dimension of our experience of food and eating. We have been talking so far about the relationship between mother (or primary caregiver) and child in relation to food. Although that is an extremely important dimension of our experience, it is only part of it. There is the whole issue of the meaning of food in our family. What were food and mealtimes used for in our households?

The Jardine family were noisy, boisterous and numerous. Their mealtimes were times of exuberant conversation during which they competed with one another for conversational space. They kept open house and the children's friends frequently came and joined in these highspirited occasions. Kate, their mother, was an exceptionally good cook and produced, apparently without undue effort, large quantities of good food. Leonard, their father, was a supportive and appreciative husband who frequently thanked his wife for the excellent food that all of them had just enjoyed. For the Jardines mealtimes were joyful opportunities for celebration. This is not to say that they did not have their sorrows or their quarrels, but mealtimes were often happy occasions.

Interestingly enough, the Jardines were all slightly overweight, as if the pleasures of eating and mealtimes were too good to resist, but none of them appeared to mind. Perhaps this can support what I am trying to say about the use of food. If you use food to celebrate as the Jardines did and in the process get rather plump, that is only an issue if it makes you unhappy. If you enjoy the way you use food, there is no problem.

The Knight family, on the other hand, had dismal and frightening mealtimes. The father of the family, Malcolm, was a violent and evil-tempered man who terrorised his wife Nora and their children. Mealtimes were when he chose to pick on his family for their table manners, their clothes, what they said or the way they said it, the expression on their faces, anything or nothing. Many, many mealtimes ended with violent rages from Malcolm and tears from a member of the family. The daughter of the family, Olivia, dealt with this situation by spending as much time as possible away from home. When she had to be part of the family she would often eat very quickly, as did her brother, apparently in an attempt to bring the meal to an end as soon as possible. Sometimes, however, the tension made it hard for her to eat and she would have times of eating very little.

As an adult Olivia found herself repeating exactly this pattern. Tension, distress or upset would provoke either a lot of rapid and rather uncontrolled eating or an anorexic episode during which she would eat very little. It was exceedingly difficult for her to establish a regular, normal pattern of eating and her weight fluctuated accordingly.

Patrick was brought up by his elderly grandparents. They were devoted to him but continued a pattern of existence that had been established for years and into which, as a late and unexpected arrival on the scene, he was never really integrated. Throughout his schooldays he ate alone. He would come home from school at the end of the day and be given his meal to eat alone. There would be nothing wrong with the food but Patrick found it difficult to concentrate on eating it. He said that he always felt as if he wanted to be out playing with his friends. His grandmother did not keep him company while he ate; it was an occasion without any kind of emotional attraction. Patrick found it extremely difficult to force himself to eat when he moved away from home. His weight was well below normal and he experienced a continual revulsion from food. However, when he began to form close relationships and to discover the pleasure of shared meals he began to be alive to how he had been continuing his family tradition with his solitary reluctant eating.

Roberta lived alone with her mother who was a nurse and worked on the night shift. She had a close and even rather clinging relationship with her mother and very few friends, so that she was accustomed to spending her evenings at home. When she came in her mother had already left for work so Roberta made her own supper and ate it in front of the television. She was lonely and hungry for her mother, but she disguised these facts from herself by turning on the television and spending the evening comforting herself with food. As she said, 'I just sit in front of the television and never notice how much I'm putting in my mouth.'

Mr and Mrs Simpson, an elderly couple, lived a life that was very unstimulating and boring. They were disappointed in life generally, which seemed to them to have been a series of hazards and crises only narrowly avoided. They saw the world outside their front door as full of danger, so they felt safer at home living a limited but reliable routine. In this routine, food assumed great importance: the planning, shopping, cooking, eating and clearing up occupied a large part of the day and their energies. This process had been going on for many years so that Mrs Simpson had steadily eaten herself to a very large size. In order to control the resulting hypertension, heart disease and numerous other side effects of her weight, she took large quantities of drugs, which in turn produced unpleasant side effects of their own. But to the doctor's suggestion that she lose weight she responded only that she was too old, that it didn't matter, and that in any case she ate very little. 'After all,' she remarked to her husband, 'what else is there to live for?'

Mealtimes serve very different purposes in different households and form part of our experience of food. None of these examples may exactly match your own experience, but perhaps thinking about them will enable you to identify what mealtimes were for you in your family and whether you are continuing, or want to continue, that pattern and tradition.

Food in your family

 This exercise will probably take you at least half an hour. You might like to do it with someone else so that you can compare experiences.

– Think about yourself as a child at a time when you can remember a fair bit about what went on, preferably before age 11.

– Think about yourself at an age when you can remember where you were living and, specifically, can remember the room in which your family (or the people you were living with) ate its meals. (If you can't remember anything from that period, choose whatever time is the earliest you can remember.)

- Draw a diagram of the room in which the meals were taken, putting in the people, the furniture, the television, the dog and any other important things that were there.
- Label the people.
- Answer the following questions:

1. In your situation – who cooked the food or made the meals?
2. What did that person feel about those jobs and in what kind of spirit did they approach them?
   - Did they like them?
   - Did they resent them?
   - Did they feel that that was what they *wanted* to do or what they *had* to do?
3. Who was the food in the family prepared for? (I know a family where the food is made for the father. It's what he wants and likes that decides what the family eats. If he isn't there they eat completely different food.)
   - Who was the important eater?
   - Was it the children?
   - Was it one of the adults?
4. What do you think the emotional purpose of mealtimes was in your situation?
   - What was supposed to happen there?
   - What was not supposed to happen?
   - Was it an opportunity for everybody to quarrel?
   - Was it an opportunity for the parents to be evil tempered with each other?
   - Was it an opportunity to bully the children?

- Was it an opportunity to have a nice time together and share the events of the day?
- Was it an opportunity to say nothing, or to make sure that nothing was said, e.g. by having the television on?

5. Look at the diagram and think about each person in turn.
   - What might each person be saying and to whom?
   - What would be said to you, and what would you say, if anything?
   - Write those things on the diagram.

6. What was your feeling memory of these occasions?
   - What sort of an occasion was it for you?
   - What sorts of things went on that you remember?

7. When you think about all of this – do you think that what went on at mealtimes was a picture of what went on in the family as a whole?
   - Do you think it is an illustration of the relationships in the family?
   - Was that how your family behaved generally?

10. Do you think you had any power?

11. Who did have power?
   - How did you feel doing the exercise?
   - What kind of memories did it trigger for you?
   - What were those feelings?
   - Can you see any connections between what went on in your family of origin at mealtimes and the way you use and think about food now?

This exercise can be very powerful. Some people find it upsetting when they revisit the memories of mealtimes that were unpleasant. Others recognise that they have repeated a pattern of behaviour in adult life that they didn't like as a child but still continue. Other people realise that their current attitude to food has been strongly influenced by that early experience. Thinking about these things can be painful but it also gives us more power to choose in the present. While we repeat the patterns of the past without even recognising it, we are the prisoners of those patterns. Seeing them gives us space to think about them and maybe to change them.

However, food also has a meaning in families over and above what mealtimes represent. Deprivation of food, for example, is commonly used as a punishment. It can be an experience which lasts a lifetime. A woman in her fifties told me over and over again the story of the supper party held by her parents to which the children of the family were allowed to come. As the youngest child she was indulged when she began to entertain the company, but her tricks went on too long, her charm ceased to amuse and her entertainment ended in her being sent to bed without any supper. At a distance of 50 years that punishment still had power to sting.

A much younger woman, Antonia, had considerably harsher treatment to deal with. Her mother had died when she was only eight years old and her father was emotionally very ill-equipped to take care of four small children, of whom Antonia was the eldest. His methods of dealing with them were extremely unpleasant. Starvation was one of them. For trivial offences Antonia would be locked in her room for days. Only her father's wealth and position in the community protected him from prosecution for ill-treatment of his children. Antonia was unable to deal with food in a relaxed way. As a child she had stolen food both at home, where it was kept under lock and key, and from shops. A severe but short-lived few months as an anorexic at the age of 16 and 17 were followed by several years of very troubled eating behaviour.

For a while things would be all right and then Antonia would be tormented by the urge to binge. In these ways she could find herself overtaken by her past.

Perhaps more commonly than deprivation of food being used as a punishment, food can be used as a comfort. Many mothers comfort their children with a sweet when they fall down. Dentists have mostly turned to comforting their young patients with stickers rather than sweets, but some doctors still hand out a sweet after an injection. Perhaps it is no wonder that we even have the phrase 'comfort eating' to describe this kind of consolation. The 'comfort' for grown people is not so much for physical hurts as for emotional pain, not so much for hurt knees as for hurt feelings.

And of course food is used as a reward and as a bribe. Sometimes when I have worked with people with eating disorders we have together devised reward systems to help them achieve changes in their eating behaviour. One of the great difficulties has been for these clients to find rewards for themselves which were not food. This is the cluster of feelings so accurately identified in the advertisement for cream cakes: 'Naughty but nice'. We are so thoroughly caught up in this way of seeing food that we give it all kinds of meanings. Two women were chatting at a social occasion when they were offered pieces of 'millionaire's shortbread', shortbread covered with toffee and chocolate. One woman refused it on the grounds that it was immoral. Shortbread, she said, should not be covered with all that stuff. It was bad enough on its own, but with a topping like that it was morally offensive. Her companion, taking a piece, said that it was impossible for a biscuit to have moral value. A biscuit could not be good or bad. Can it?

The reward/bribe system works at a number of levels in our society. Business circles use it a great deal. Directors' dining rooms, expense account lunches and dinners, Christmas parties for the staff, these are all part of it. In fact, eating and food have become so important in our society that they confer status and importance. And of course where food is plentiful, as it is in our society, then all kinds of subtle meanings become attached to what is eaten when. We are none of us immune to all of this. The immense number of opportunities to eat, the endless attempts to titillate our jaded palates with new combinations or new ideas, all combine to push us further and further away from the capacity to listen to our bodies' needs and supply them appropriately.

Take, for example, the confectionery industry's attempts to get us to eat their products. They present us with the most extravagant rewards and associations to tempt us to put into our bodies something that has no nutritional value, indeed something which may well rob our bodies of nutrients. It is indicated to us that we will be socially and sexually successful. We will be beautiful. We will be young. We will be rich and leisured. Many of us are not able to resist these blandishments. That is what is intended and hoped for.

Current Patterns of Eating

It is now more than 60 years since the end of the Second World War, but in our (western European) society there are still large numbers of people who remember rationing. It is now a nutritionist's commonplace to say that rationing was the best thing that ever happened to Britain because it obliged people to eat in a relatively healthy way. It was, however, not a matter of choice. As anyone will tell you who remembers those times, nobody got fat during rationing. There was a strict limit on calorie intake imposed by scarcity.

If we think about the era before the Second World War we are recalling times preceding the advent of the welfare state, before the increased prosperity that we enjoy now, when there was widespread poverty and acute hunger. There were great inequalities in society and food was not as plentiful in the sense of being within the financial reach of all.

It is then only in the last 50 years or so that our society has been as glutted with food as it is now, with the consequent great pressures to eat. Our culture has become accustomed to abundant and inexpensive food supplies being reliably available 24/7. The relative cost of food has declined rapidly. Around 1900, families in the UK could expect to spend 50 per cent of their income on food. Around 1950 that figure was about 30 per cent; around 1980 it was 20 per cent. Now it is about 10 per cent. Yet we have not adapted to this plenty.

Our eating patterns have changed radically. Take a couple of small examples. Fifty years ago it was unusual to see people eating and drinking on the streets and in public places. Now it is the norm. Similarly, not so long ago eating between meals, even if it was a common enough activity, was thought to be a bad idea. Now for increasing numbers of people there are no established mealtimes and changes in the food industry have eroded established patterns of what to eat. The phenomenon known as 'grazing' is upon us where it is normal to eat all day long in an unstructured way and without much reference to time of day. The old certainties of how much of what to eat when are disappearing. For those of us whose inner psychological certainty about food has been damaged, the trackless territory of contemporary eating behaviour creates tremendous problems. Interestingly enough, programmes for recovering food misusers often include a requirement to eat in a thoroughly conventional way at fixed mealtimes, so that in one dimension at least there is some guidance.

Some western European countries — perhaps France, Spain, Italy, maybe others — seem to the casual observer at least to have suffered less disintegration in family structures than Britain or the USA. In these countries meals seem a much more important family occasion and to have retained formal and ritual value. This may perhaps help those who otherwise might lose their bearings completely about food and hunger. In France, for example, the obesity rate is exactly half of what it is in the UK.[5]

Quite apart from the personal and inner difficulties with food, society as a whole has not adapted well to the constant availability and abundance of food. So far as I am aware, no society has. North America has had to deal with this situation longer than western Europe; the difficulties created have started earlier and chart a path that we seem to be following.

However, it could only be in a society in which food was so immensely important that eating disorders would make sense. This is very obviously the case with anorexia. To put it crudely, if you are anorexic in a society in which many people are underfed then you are not so remarkable, but to starve in a society of overfed people is something very different. This is equally true of obesity. In a society where food is in short supply, then to be fat is a signal of the power to choose to eat when that power is not general. It therefore conveys wealth or status within the society. Where we all have the opportunity to overeat, the fact that only some do gives that gesture emotional meaning and significance. If, more strangely, people eat and then get rid of the food so that it cannot nourish them, they make an even more violent statement.

This chapter has shown how our personal experience and the society in which we live supply us with a context for our eating behaviour. This experience does not necessarily turn us into food misusers, but does give us a language, a way of behaving, if we get to the point of feeling that we have to use it. It gives us weapons, ammunition of a certain kind, if we need to take them up. What I now want to go on to explore is what reasons there might be for us to be taking up these very powerful weapons.

Part II

Chapter Three
Disordered Eating as a Response to Crisis

"This [behaviour in crisis] was a temporary hitch in a reasonably well-managed life."
— Ellen Noonan, *Counselling Young People*, 1983

In Chapter 1 I described the process by which a child develops a secure attachment to her main caregivers and how the care she receives in a good situation becomes the care that she can offer to herself (and to others). Part of the process of developing as an adult is to be able to repeat the pattern of care that you have received even when you are no longer living with your family of origin. So we expect young people to be able to make the transition from life at home with parents to a semi-independent life as adults (perhaps away at college) and then eventually to independent adult life. We also expect them to be able to manage new situations and new feelings. When attachment experience has been good – that is to say when a young person is securely attached – these challenges can usually be managed relatively easily. We expect our youngsters to come home for weekends, especially when they first leave home, but we also expect them to gradually find their new life more interesting and more rewarding and to come home less often. However, when a new situation is experienced as too different or too frightening, those secure beginnings may not be enough and a youngster may find the need to manage the situation with food.

We use our emergency ways of coping when we feel most under stress or threat. One of the commonest and most obvious of these situations is when a girl leaves home for the first time. Very often this move to college or to her own place is accompanied by a quite considerable weight gain or loss. This is such a frequent occurrence that there is a whole series of common-sense reasons produced to explain it: the food in the canteen is stodgy; she doesn't like the food they give her; she's eating too much fast food instead of cooking for herself; she's not eating a balanced diet; she doesn't know how to cook properly; the cooking facilities aren't very good; she has to share the kitchen with so many other people; she's a vegetarian and the hostel gives her such boring vegetarian food – and so on.

Yet it seems that for many young people leaving home for the first time is an especially difficult moment in their lives. It doesn't help that it is probably something they wanted to do with a sizeable chunk of themselves, that they were thoroughly fed up with living at home and very conscious of its problems and disadvantages. They expected to be able to make a painless transition into independent living and very probably other people expected it of them too: 'You'll be looking forward to getting a place of your own . . . I expect you're looking forward to doing your own thing . . . You'll be glad to get away to college.' Of course, for many there are these feelings, but they are not as simple and unmixed as other people seem to expect, or as they expect of themselves.

What is being referred to here is the ordinary anxiety about transition from being an adolescent living at home to being a young adult establishing her own independence. It does not refer to the much more serious difficulties to be discussed later of those eating disorders that are the effect of serious and long-standing problems in making the transition from child to adolescent to adult. However, because these more short-lived difficulties are not so serious, it does not mean that they are not painful.

Fiona's Story

Fiona got herself a place at a college in London a long way from her family home. Her family lived in a quiet, remote part of the country and there enjoyed a quiet, rather old-fashioned and conservative life. Fiona was herself a rather quiet, conservative, old-fashioned girl. However, with part of herself at least, she obviously wanted something more exciting or she would never have contemplated so radical a move. The reality of living and going to college in London was horrifying to her. She was appalled by the way her fellow students spoke and behaved. She was shocked by their bad language, their sexually explicit conversations and their casual overindulgence in alcohol and use of drugs. She was threatened by their active sexuality, by the self-confidence, as she saw it, the pushiness, of some of the students. She felt there was almost no one like her and her obvious disapproval and contempt for her fellow students certainly did not help her to make friends. She could survive in an alienated kind of way while she was actually attending her classes, but when she went home to her student hostel she fell apart.

The band-aid with which she chose to cover her wounds was food. Evening after evening she would sit on her own in the deserted kitchen of the hostel eating bread and butter, for her the symbolic food of childhood and of home. By half-term she had gained a stone in weight and lost a ton in confidence and self-esteem. She suffered worst from agonies of homesickness and it was this feeling in particular that she tried to anaesthetise with food. With dogged courage she stuck out most of the first year of her course. It was only when she began to accept that it was no disgrace to be homesick that she could allow herself to consider other courses and other colleges nearer home.

There was nothing wrong with Fiona's development as an adolescent, but she had made a change that was more than she was ready for at the time. When she could feel that she need not be ashamed of her feelings, she did not need to try to obliterate them with bread and butter, but instead could begin to make plans that were more appropriate to her temperament and her emotional development.

Stop and Think

Think about the transitions in your life – perhaps from school to college, living at home to living away, studying to working, being single to being in a relationship, living on your parents' money to earning your own, living with your family to living with someone else, being married to being divorced or bereaved. How do you think those transitions have affected you? Is there a specific transition that has been especially difficult for you? Do you think that it has affected your eating behaviour? What kind of support did you need, or do you need now, to help you manage that transition better?

Time to Mourn

In Fiona's situation there had been some emotional work left undone, very possibly emotional work for which there was no encouragement or opportunity. That emotional work is the work of grieving. Most of us think about our lives as progress (at least to middle age) towards something better. The advantages of being older and more grown up than in fact we are appear constantly before our eyes. This applies not only to the natural urge for physical mastery and maturity – co-ordination, physical strength, height, weight – but also in adolescents to social mastery. The freedoms to smoke, drink, stay up late, drive, go out without adults, have sexual experience, see adult films, earn more money are very seductively displayed and make it difficult sometimes for us to allow ourselves to be the age we are emotionally and chronologically. One effect of this, then, is that it is hard to mourn for the pleasures of the part of our life that we are leaving behind. Peter Pan gets very little sympathy these days, yet I suspect there are many who entered puberty and adolescence with a pang for what they were leaving behind.

There is a similar story to be told at the point of transition from adolescence to young adulthood. To express sadness at leaving home – sadness that a whole part of our life with our parents is over – is not always very easy. The cultural climate does not encourage it. But nevertheless the evidence is that such natural mourning is not an optional extra but a necessary and desirable part of our capacity to take up the challenges of the next stage of our development.

Similarily the transitions from being single to being a couple, from life without obligations to parenthood and paying the mortgage are not always simple. These are adult responsibilities to which the child part of ourselves – that bit of ourselves that feels strongly and even irrationally – can respond with dismay or even regret.

Denise's Story

Denise was 27 years old when she first really put on weight. She had got married three years before and had hugely enjoyed setting up house and living together with her partner. They had established themselves in a flat and created a routine that suited them both. David, Denise's husband, worked in an office some miles from home and Denise worked in the local nursery. Denise was very fond of children and not surprisingly she and David decided to start a family. When she was 26 she had a healthy baby girl. This meant that she stopped working for a bit and decided that she would not return to work until the baby went to nursery herself. To her great surprise she started to find being at home as a mother much more difficult than she had imagined. The baby seemed to take all her time and energy so that she found the ordinary housekeeping a problem and felt she had very little time to see her friends or socialise with other mums. Denise's mum lived a long way away and couldn't be there on a daily basis to help and support her. She might have become depressed but you can't really be depressed about having a beautiful baby, can you? So she hid her feelings from herself and everybody else by snacking throughout the day. She excused herself to other people by saying that she was finding it difficult to lose the weight she had gained when she had the baby, but in fact she was steadily gaining weight. Fortunately, she had a very sympathetic health visitor who noticed that she was putting on weight and asked her how she was feeling. To her own surprise and embarrassment Denise burst into tears and poured out the story of her feelings of incompetence. Her health visitor was extremely helpful when she reminded Denise that she would need time to adjust to the huge change that had taken place in her life. She also recommended that Denise should talk things over more with her husband, who had no real idea how she felt. With these two simple pieces of advice Denise was able to recognise the need for support in a new situation and to allow herself some regret for the carefree pre-parental life she had left behind. When she joined the parent support group in her GP surgery, she found that she wasn't the only one who missed getting up late at the weekend or the social life around work. New friends and renewed confidence soon returned her eating to normal and her weight to what it had been before.

Food and Relationships

Another area of crisis is that of relationships. It is very common for women who use food in crisis to binge or starve when relationships go wrong – especially love relationships. Again we are talking about the ordinary ups and downs that are part of the process of looking for a long-term partner, not the more serious eating disorders (to be discussed later) where those who find it exceedingly difficult to form relationships at all may use eating disorders as a holding pattern to keep the whole issue at a distance. However, the 'ordinariness' of such crises in no way diminishes their capacity to cause a lot of pain.

Iris's Story

Take, for example, the story of Iris, a lively, clever, funny, popular girl who lived an extremely busy, active social life. One of the reasons she was so popular was that she was always good-tempered, always smiling. When she split up with her boyfriends, she didn't feel it bothered her. She got a bit upset, that was all: easy come, easy go. Her sadness soon passed and she was her old self again.

But underneath this jolly coping self was a girl who dealt with the crises with the men in her life by eating. This fact she kept secret even from herself for a long time, although she was upset by her inability to keep her weight down. She did not know in any sort of conscious way what she was doing. Anyway, this system hadn't worked too badly for about three years, so why should she know? But one autumn she broke up with a boy that she had really liked. Her weight increased. She began not to cope at work. She started taking a lot of time off and became depressed. Depression was something new in her life. As far as she could remember, she had never felt so miserable before. It was sufficiently alarming for her to seek help, particularly because, as she said, nothing was wrong in her life. She didn't know what she was depressed about. As far as she was concerned it had just happened to her.

Gradually, as she began to try to remember when she got depressed and what had been happening in her life at that time, it became obvious to her that she had been upset by the break-up with her boyfriend. But that was a puzzle to her because she didn't get upset about boyfriends. Then, without recognising the connection, Iris began to talk about the real problem in her life: her failure to control her weight and eating. Soon she began to see the connection. Maybe she didn't consciously get upset, but certainly something was hurting inside when she stuffed herself with food. Then we began to talk about her family and how they dealt with crisis. The answer was that they didn't. No one was allowed to get upset, particularly not Iris. Her mother insisted that Iris always presented a smiling face and had been known to hang up on her if her telephone calls were not sufficiently upbeat.

In fact, Iris's problems with food were quite an ingenious way of dealing with distress that she had never learned to express more openly. However, it was a system that had not proved strong enough to cope with a really painful loss. Her pain had emerged as depression and disordered eating. How was she going to do it differently?

There were lots of things going for Iris. One was that, although she had a family and a mother who had difficulties in dealing with crisis, she was fortunate that her childhood had been good. She was securely attached and a much loved and cared for child. So she was not a young woman in crisis trying to deal with a not very good beginning, as so many of those to be described in this book have had to do. If you like, all she needed was to be helped to find a way to respond more directly to her relationships with men. Second, she badly wanted to be rid of her problems with food. She wanted to lose weight and become as beautiful as undoubtedly she would be. She was tired of fighting herself about food all the time. So she was well motivated to try a different way of doing it. Third, although she was scared of feeling her pain, she was not very, very scared. Somewhere inside her there was a very strong, capable person (carefully nurtured by her parents) who was tough enough to survive a lot.

When we had reached this point in our discussions, I didn't see Iris for several weeks. When she came back she told me this story. She had been going on a trip with a boy who was a close friend. They were looking for the place they wanted to visit, but by mistake took a wrong turning in the car. The anxiety and frustration of the situation made Iris cry, and once started she found it hard to stop. Her friend asked her how he could help and she told him that she wanted him to take her home to his flat. This he did and he stayed with her, taking care of her. She cried for almost three days, over all the things she had not cried about for three years. She said that during those three days she realised what a lot she had not felt and how much feeling there was to do. She said that it had been awful and terrible, but in a positive kind of way, and that she had felt incredibly much better since.

One of the remarkable things about this story is how, once given permission, Iris knew exactly what she needed to do. What's more, she could find the time and the occasion, the safe person and the safe place. Without consciously planning it, she had supplied herself with a very good opportunity to catch up on her backlog of emotional work.

Undoubtedly this is not the end of the story. Human beings don't change as fast as that. However, there has been a remarkable shift in Iris's ability to express her feelings directly. With support and encouragement there is a good chance of a lasting change. At the same time Iris's eating disorder has shrunk from being a monster to being a default position that she can recognise. When Iris wants to overeat these days, she is beginning to be able to stop and ask herself the question: 'What's upsetting me today?'

Exactly the same mechanism at work with Iris is acted out with people whose tendency is to anorexia or to bulimia rather than to compulsive eating. When things go badly in their intimate relationships, they starve themselves or binge. This is not to be confused with the changes in eating behaviour that often go with grief and mourning. The anorexia and bulimia are instead of grief and mourning; they actually prevent any grieving and mourning. Grieving and mourning is an acknowledgement of emotional needs, hungers, dependencies, a process by which it is possible to come to terms with loss. It is that pain of need and loss that not eating is intended to abolish.

Stop and Think
- How do you manage your love relationships?
- Are you someone who deals with the ups and downs or the end of relationships by turning to (or away from) food?
- How could you manage that pain better?
- How could you soothe yourself without using food (or anything else that isn't good for you)?
- Can you find a way to talk to yourself kindly?
- Who could you talk to who would listen and support you?

Responding to Unexpected Trauma

Even securely attached and confident people can find themselves overwhelmed by events that are more than they know how to cope with. Manjit worked in the kiosk of a garage. She was on duty when the kiosk was raided by men wearing balaclavas and waving baseball bats. Not surprisingly, she was utterly terrified, so frightened that she wet herself. Her colleague handed over the cash and the raiders left without hurting anyone, but Manjit was absolutely traumatised. The police soon came and she then had to make a statement in a process that took hours. When it was all over she went home. That evening and for some time afterwards Manjit had flashbacks to the raid. She felt completely unable to return to work and didn't even want to leave the house. Her family and her boyfriend were very shocked to hear what had happened and supported her very well, but of course they had to go to work. Manjit was left alone during the day. She discovered that she felt a little better if she took her mind off things by just watching television or listening to music; it also helped if she soothed herself by drinking hot chocolate and eating biscuits. Initially, Manjit's employers were very understanding and allowed her to take time off, but after about ten days they started to let her know that they expected her to return to work. At that point Manjit had still not been outside the house and had put on half a stone in weight. Fortunately, she had an excellent GP. She went to see him and was able to tell him, with many tears, just how terrified she had felt and how she was now nervous about unexpected sounds and frightened to go to sleep at night. The GP gave her some medication to help her feel less anxious and referred her for some crisis counselling, which luckily she could access the same week. Almost immediately she began to feel better, was able to go back to work and over a few weeks stopped soothing herself with food. Manjit was fundamentally a secure and strong young woman who with help and support could deal with even the really horrible experience of the raiders. However, in that crisis she had temporarily turned to food. When she felt better she could let it go and return to her normal eating patterns and her normal weight.

Eating Your Worries Away

Lastly there is disordered eating which arises as a response to 'worry'. If a woman puts on weight or loses it, there's a common-or-garden, everyday, kind of explanation often right at hand: 'Oh, she's been worried.' However, a more accurate description might be: 'She was trying not to worry.' Everyone has lots of things to worry about – money, exams, relationships, work, families. Many people lead complicated, busy lives, trying to respond to all sorts of demands. Often a solution to all this pressure is to try to obliterate the worry with food or starvation, rather than to think about what is causing the worry.

There is, that is to say, a positive and creative form of worrying, a necessary and desirable form of worrying – 'worry work'. Of course it is possible to worry in a way that prevents any emotional work being done. We can revolve endlessly and pointlessly in our heads about the things that bother us. This is the kind of worrying that gets us nowhere – the worrying whether the back door is locked, the worry whether the house is tidy enough, the worry about money and paying the bills. We can worry about them without ever really tackling the subject of our worries. But there is another form of worry that is valuable and necessary. If I'm lying in bed worrying whether the back door is locked, then I should get out of bed and look. That kind of worry – of appropriate concern – pushes us into doing what we actually need to do. It is this sort of creative worrying that we can fail to do if we use food to prevent it.

Take a common enough situation – a young woman is due to take an examination in two days time. She's worried about it, but she doesn't let herself worry creatively. Instead, she sits down with her books, a packet of biscuits and a cup of coffee. She's so distracted by the biscuits, their smell and the look of them that she can't concentrate. She feels she shouldn't have one, but she does and then she wants more. She eats them, one by one, feeling so guilty that she can't concentrate. She's worrying, in a pointless kind of way, about her examination, but she's also using food to stop herself worrying. If she worked at her worry she would know she needs to revise one set of notes tonight and another set tomorrow night and then she might have a chance of passing her examination. At the moment she thinks she's working but really she's wondering whether she should make herself sick because she's eaten a whole packet of biscuits and if she goes on like this she'll be as fat as a pig.

It can go the other way, of course. A woman is going for an interview and decides that she won't get the job until she's thinner. She's so confused about the difference between 'herself' and her appearance that she is trying to improve her chances of getting the job by being thinner. So then she spends the next ten days worrying about weight and food and size and calories and not thinking at all about how to present 'herself' at the interview and researching the company. This is a shame because in order to do well at the interview she needs to spend time preparing her thoughts and ideas. In fact she needs to work at it, but she doesn't. She stops herself from doing necessary worry work and instead focuses on how much she's eating.

Stop and Think

How do you respond to the things that worry you? What is the most familiar thing for you to worry about? Do you think you use food to try and manage your worries? How could you deal with them more directly? Who could you turn to who might be able to advise you and help you?

This is not by any means an exhaustive list of the crises that people may meet in their lives, but it is enough to illustrate the point. Our eating behaviour may cause us little difficulty except in crisis, and then we can suddenly find ourselves bingeing or starving. If we can permit ourselves to make the link between what is going on in our lives and what we are doing with food, we may be able to tolerate our eating behaviour in the short term, but also look for other ways of coping.

Chapter Four
On Being a Woman

"It is the thesis of this book that compulsive eating in women is a response to their social position."
— Susie Orbach, *Fat is a Feminist Issue*, 2006

The associations produced by food, the memories and the history of our experience with food that were discussed in Chapter 2 are, of course, not just the property of women. We all, male and female, have a lifetime of eating to remember. However, eating disorders are, very largely, a women's complaint. (However, men have a chapter to themselves later in this book.) Why is that? Part of the answer may be that women tend to express their distress in ways that hurt themselves rather than turning it out and against other people. However, the question has been answered further by feminist writers and this chapter takes a look at some aspects of their understanding of why women are so tormented by issues of size, of food and of eating.

Morag's Story

Morag's initial complaint was not that she had difficulties with food but that she was depressed. When she began to talk about her life it didn't seem very surprising. Here was a healthy young woman of 20 living a life of such monotony and boredom that she had every right to be depressed. Morag was a student in her second year at university, surrounded on every side by the attractions and stimulus not only of her studies and the student community, but by the cultural and social riches of London.

Amid this plenty Morag lived a rigid and undeviating routine. She got up at the same time, ate her meals at the same time, studied at the same place in the same library at the same time every day. Weekends caused her great anxiety because the structure of her life was not so rigidly provided by lectures and tutorials, so she performed her domestic chores, such as doing her laundry and cleaning her room in the student hostel, with the undeviating regularity with which she attended classes. A tiny indication that there might be another Morag hidden somewhere beneath this mass of rules and regulations was provided by her membership of a church choir. But even this activity was undertaken with the same relentless routine as the rest of her life.

Morag was also considerably overweight and dressed in a parody of middle-aged fashion. Probably her dress style was modelled on her mother's, but in any case it conveyed a woman whose sense of her own possibilities of being physically attractive was very much damaged. In fact she looked a boring frump. Gradually, as we talked, more details emerged of Morag's way of life and of her sadness and despair. She had some female friends at the church she attended and occasionally went out with them. Similarly, she had found another woman friend at her hostel. The pair of them used to meet each evening at 10 pm to drink hot chocolate before bedtime at 10.30. Part of Morag stoutly defended this way of living. She found academic work difficult so she needed lots of time to study; she needed to copy out her lecture notes each day, it was her way of learning. She didn't want to go out in the evenings – it made her too tired the next day. She didn't want to go to parties as crowds of people made her anxious. Besides, sometimes she did go to films with her friends.

But with another part of her Morag was lonely, unhappy and dissatisfied. She was particularly concerned about her weight and size. 'If only,' she constantly said, 'if only I was thinner I wouldn't feel so bad. I wouldn't mind going out if I didn't feel as if everyone was looking at me, thinking "God, she's fat".' Gradually she was able to tell me about her struggles with food and how she sometimes spent the weekend in a frenzy of misery.

What was it all about? What was her attachment history? In time Morag was able to tell me about her family, and then the picture became a little clearer. Her father was a bully and a drunkard who terrorised his wife and two children. He was capable of violent rages, especially if some detail of the domestic arrangements failed to please him. Morag's mother was a drudge in this household, afraid of her husband and abused by him. He had many ways of maintaining his tyranny, not least of which had been to deprive his family of money. Morag's mother had focused her energies on trying to protect the girls from him.

Not surprisingly, Morag had been glad to escape from this environment and her diligence at school had enabled her to do so via university. However, once there she hardly knew what to do with herself. She had no experience of socialising because she had always been forbidden by her father to go out at night, or to bring friends home. She did not know how to relax and enjoy herself because, in order to survive, as a schoolgirl she had created a rigid programme of attending to her homework. The undeviating regime she had created at university was her way of continuing this protective system.

But at the same time in some corner of her head Morag knew that there was more to life than the way she was living it. She was curious about boys, but at the same time very frightened of them. In her first year at university she had been invited to the freshers' ball, but in total panic had refused the invitation. Since then, however, these anxieties had been overtaken by a constant anxiety about her size. Over and over again she told me that if only she could get thin her problems would be over.

In due course Morag began to talk about what she might do once she had her degree. She told me that she thought she would like children, but she added she didn't think she wanted a husband, or even a boyfriend. In fact she had wondered if she could make use of the services of a sperm bank. What was it, I wondered aloud to her, that was so unattractive about living with a man. And then out of Morag's mouth came a torrent of words about how horrible men are, how mean, how selfish, how cruel, how unloving. And for a woman to live with a man, I asked? She was a slave, said Morag, taken advantage of, used, a victim. She was much better off on her own.

Morag's understanding of relationships between men and women was hardly surprising. This was the pattern she knew and could imagine no other. Seventy-five per cent of us repeat the attachment patterns of our childhood. This is fine if you're attachment experience is good and you have a history of secure and loving relationships; you will find it relatively easy to choose a partner who will be kind and loving. But for those who have less fortunate attachment experience, choosing is as likely to follow the pattern they know. Modern research has confirmed, for at least some of us, the old story that boys marry their mothers and girls marry their fathers. Morag was terrified of choosing her father.

Morag did not consciously know that she was describing her parents and the relationship between them. Like most of us she assumed that her experience was how it was for everyone. More than most of us, she had had little opportunity for discovering that it could be different. Unconsciously she was convinced that any relationship with a man would place her in the same situation that her mother had been in. Morag's life might be limited, but she was not the exploited slave that her mother had become. Her size, her appearance, her way of life and her preoccupation with food were all a way of protecting herself from her mother's fate. She thought of herself as afraid of men and of their sexual impulses, but she was also afraid of her own sexual feelings because they ran the risk of getting her involved with a man.

When Morag began to realise where her image of the role of women came from, she began to be able to think about the possibility that there might be other ways of relating to men than the one she saw her mother engaged in. She could begin to think what sort of relationship she might like. As she became less afraid and more hopeful she began to find her problems with food less compulsive and she began to lose weight.

Perhaps Morag represents an extreme example of a woman's rejection of the role of woman presented to her by society. But even if her experience of what it means to be a woman was particularly unpalatable, it provides, I think, a rather good example of how women will use compulsive eating as a protest against being sexual on other people's terms and as a preoccupation that enables us to push down our sexual feelings. It is very hard to carry on a relationship if you are preoccupied with what you eat, what shape you are and how much you weigh.

Stop and Think

– What is your image of life with a sexual partner?
– Do you think that image is a mirror of the relationship between your parents?
– If you have consciously tried to find a sexual partner with whom the dynamic is different from the way it was between your parents, how successful have you been?
– Do you find that you fall in love with people who are not good for you?
– Have you thought of using a tick list of desirable qualities to guide you, rather than allowing your feelings to be your only guide?

Thin is Beautiful?

Let us look at this idea a little more closely. What it suggests is that there is a 'received', accepted shape for a woman to be if she wants to be viewed as a sexual person. Hilde Bruch,[1] in her work on anorexia, named 'fashion' as one of the pressures which urge women towards being thin, and in anorexia gets completely out of hand. Indeed, the history of fashion is the history of how different parts of the female body have been emphasised at different times and required to be of a certain size and shape.

Think for a moment of the images of women presented to us and the multitude of means of doing so. The advertising industry depicts women on television, on billboards, in magazines and in newspapers. By these endless visual images we are shown women whose sexual success, attractiveness, wealth, leisure, beauty and youth are all associated with being thin – and of course with whatever product is being promoted.

Yet considering all the money and pressure from inside and out, not to mention the time, concern and worry, we seem to make an extraordinarily poor job of keeping thin. Large numbers of women (and men) are carrying considerably more weight than their frames can manage comfortably, let alone more than the advertising industry decrees. What is more, if we do succeed in getting rid of the extra weight, what do we do but put it straight back on again? Various studies all point to the same conclusion – that very few people maintain weight loss even for one year.[2]

The failure to achieve or maintain weight loss is, of course, put down to lack of persistence, lack of willpower, lack of moral fibre, and so on. What feminists have done is to turn this on its head and say that maybe women don't want to be thin, that maybe their continuing failure with diets and weight loss, and the way they maintain their fat with compulsive eating, is in some way intentional. Maybe fat serves a purpose for women, and maybe that purpose is to protest against the

Stop and Think

Which images from the media do you think affect you? Do you think you compare yourself with images that you see and with other people? You probably know that airbrushing can create images that are remote from reality. Does this idea help you when you look at photographs of celebrities, for instance? How important is the way you look to the sense of yourself? Can you go out without make-up or without washing your hair? Would you like to be freer of these influences?

way women's bodies are objectified and abused, and to protest against the role in society which women have been assigned.

Fat as a Message

Susie Orbach has done some extremely interesting work with women in which she has been able to get to the positive meanings that women give to their fat. Of course many of us are familiar with the routine of hating ourselves because we are fat, feeling loathing and contempt for what we put into our mouths, feeling disgust with our size and shape (however unreasonable all of that may be on any rational understanding). What is much more interesting is to identify what we might be trying to accomplish by our resolute refusal to be thin.

Orbach identifies two major purposes in the behaviour of the compulsive eater. One is power and the defiance of the impotent image of women. The other is anger. A characteristic of the physical images of women most often presented to us by the media is their physical fragility. Women are often shown (and indeed often clothe themselves) in garments that make physical comfort and exertion impossible. It is impossible to run in high heels and a tight skirt. But aside from that, women are shown without any kind of muscle development. And, of course, being thin they do not weigh very much. By this means the ordinary fact that men are usually taller, heavier and stronger is turned into a gross imbalance. Men are encouraged to physical development, exertion and competition; women are inhibited from it. With that physical fragility is often shown an intellectual incapacity. Some women actually pretend to be stupid in order to maintain an intellectual imbalance to match the physical (pretending not to know how the car works; not bothering to understand pensions or life assurance). Then with those goes a kind of emotional feebleness – women cry rather than get angry or sulk rather than say what they think.

No wonder a lot of us want to dissociate ourselves from all of this. Some of us manage to do so directly. There are far more models of strong women about – in athletics, in business, in politics – and more of us are managing to assert ourselves as women. But this is often extremely difficult within the social and cultural context in which we find ourselves, and for some of us the attempt remains indirect. The way some of us seem to have found of trying to be powerful is by increasing our bulk, by abolishing in some sort of metaphorical way our fragility, our weakness, our impotence. I once worked with a woman who told me that when she got into bed with her husband her weight made the mattress tilt, so that he was disturbed. She

Stop and Think

Could it be true for you that not getting thin is some kind of a statement? Try this as a way of exploring that possibility. Make a list of the reasons for and against losing weight. You may think that there is everything to be gained by losing weight and nothing to be lost, but maybe you will discover that there are some ways that being heavy works for you, for instance:

– Is your weight a limitation on what can be asked of you?
– Is your weight a protection against unwanted sex?
– Is eating a lot a compensation for other unsatisfactory parts of your life?
– Is eating the only thing that gives you any pleasure?

smiled when she told me this and acknowledged that it was satisfying that her weight had an effect on him.

Valerie's Story

Valerie was someone who had been sexually abused as a child. From an early age she was sexually active herself. She was a very big woman, tall, strong and heavy. Despite her size (or because of it) she was a considerable athlete and competed on equal terms with men both at squash and tennis. She was fiercely competitive and therefore a challenging opponent at these games. In due course the local male squash champion sought her out to play. Their games were hard fought but usually the man won. Valerie realised that in order to have greater speed around the court she needed to lose some weight. She duly put herself on a diet and began to lose weight. Her competitiveness and perseverance served her as well in this as in her sport. Steadily over the weeks and months she took off her weight and sure enough was speedier around the court and began to win her squash games. Then she stopped, not because she had got to the weight she had set herself, but because she began to feel less powerful, less in command, less in control. It was as if her sense of being strong, of having authority, of being someone to reckon with, was identified completely with her size. If she lost too much weight she would be vulnerable and in danger. That fear was related to her actual experience as a sexually abused child. In her sexual relationships as an adult she had refused to allow herself to be too vulnerable, too drawn in, and with men and women she had used her physical size, weight and strength to make sure she would never again, if she could help it, join the ranks of the weak and powerless. But with her size she also expressed her fury, which she could not yet feel emotionally, about how she had been exploited. Her size expressed the reality that she was and would no longer be a victim. She at least would not repeat her attachment history.

Wendy's Story

Wendy had been married for years and had delayed having a child because of her interest in her work and her developing career. However, with the biological clock ticking away, the time came to start having children if that was what she was going to do. In fact she and her husband found it very difficult to conceive. There seemed to be no biological impediment, although various medical authorities told Wendy to lose weight to bring down her blood pressure, but this she seemed to find impossible. She was considerably overweight and had been for years. But one thing was clear to Wendy – just as soon as she did have a baby she would resign from work. In the meantime, however, she found herself another job that was more rewarding and more prestigious than she had dreamed possible. She did not, however, lose weight. It began to be clear that all Wendy's anxieties about what she would lose if she had a child were expressed in her size. She looked permanently pregnant, as if to satisfy that part of her that wanted to have a child, but there was a stronger force which made her very reluctant to give up her power in the world in exchange for motherhood. Yet she had created for herself such an ideal of motherhood that she was unable to express that conflict except by her size.

Mrs Brown

Mrs Brown was the large wife of a clergyman. More than most women she was defined by her husband's job. Part of her role was to be professionally 'nice', kind and good-tempered, despite how she might really be feeling. Indeed, there seemed also to be a professional embargo on 'feeling' anything but 'nice'. Certainly Mrs Brown did not know she was anything but nice, although an acute observer might have noticed a fair number of sour comments and disparaging judgements. It was hard for her to see that she stifled her resentment at the role she had to play, her rage at the way her own considerable talents had not been allowed to develop – because of course a woman in her position couldn't go out to work. Oh no, her husband needed her too much. The only way her anger could be expressed was by the biting and swallowing of food.

There are two things to be said about compulsive eating as a way of dealing with our dissatisfaction and distress about our social role as women. The first is that it does not work. In fact it is an exceedingly painful and difficult way to live. Nobody can enjoy the craving to eat irrespective of physical need. It is an extremely painful addiction that has to be carried on in secret and is full of shame and guilt. There is something frightening and humiliating about the desperate need to eat. When it means a binge followed by vomiting and purging, then the compulsive eater finds it hard to hang on to any shred of self-esteem, let alone what it does to the way she feels physically. Alice used to come to work looking truly terrible, her face bloated, her eyes bloodshot, pale as a ghost. In the beginning her colleagues used to comment and ask her what was wrong, but her evasive replies and embarrassment soon made them stop. Alice could only imagine them speculating behind her back on what she did to make herself so ill. This worry made her keep herself apart from her workmates until she was leading an extremely isolated existence.

Not only is it a painful way to live, but it also does not begin to deal with the problem. In this chapter we have been considering the idea that compulsive eating may be a response to a woman's perception of her social role. By misusing food a woman may be making a statement about what she feels about her life as a woman. But this issue is not in any way tackled or dealt with by the eating behaviour. In fact, it is a way of not knowing about or dealing with these issues. It is a translation into eating behaviour of feelings. Those feelings may be any of a large range – fear, anger, envy, despair – but they are feelings that we evidently feel we cannot know about or deal with, that somehow have to be magicked away and only to make a reappearance as eating behaviour.

It is true, of course, that the feelings are hard to deal with. Mrs Brown had been trained for so long and so thoroughly never to know that she had an unkind or angry thought or feeling that to acknowledge that she was indeed like the rest of us was very, very hard. And also like the rest of us, Mrs Brown was very judgemental about such ideas and feelings. She thought they were bad, wicked and wrong. She was very unaccepting of herself and found it hard to distinguish between a thought or feeling which has no moral value and an action which may have moral value. So, for example, she found it difficult to take in the idea that feeling angry about the way her husband presumed she would be willing to sacrifice her life and career for his life and career might be a very appropriate response. But she was angry about it and she showed her anger in ways she did not allow herself to recognise, especially by her eating.

However, there was something else that Mrs Brown found hard to deal with, and also hid from herself with her fat and her preoccupation with food. This was the extent to which she had agreed to be her husband's deputy. She would say that of course she hadn't expected to go on working when she married a clergyman and that in fact she had been quite glad to give up work. Besides, assisting her husband in the parish was very rewarding; there were lots of people in need and it was good to be able to help out. At a deeper level though, she blamed her husband for stifling her career and her prospects and she was in some ways an embittered and unforgiving woman.

None of this was easy to deal with for Mrs Brown, nor would it be for any of us. What is more, there was no way of putting it right. She no longer had her life before her. Her opportunity to develop her career was by this time over; she was a middle-aged woman. Yet there was a lot to be gained by allowing herself to know about her true feelings. For a start she need no longer spend her days preoccupied with food and thinking about the next meal. She also had the opportunity to grow and develop as a person, as a woman, as a human being. There was emotional work that desperately needed to be done in Mrs Brown's life. There was the need to grieve for what had not happened, for the opportunities missed and the potential unrealised. There was the need to achieve a more honest relationship with her husband, to stop sniping at him indirectly and to begin to attempt to be more direct about her own feelings. Most of all there was the need for her to consider how she was going to live the last part of her life and how she could use the remaining years as creatively as possible. Compulsive eating was a way of surviving, not living.

What we have to come to terms with is that we may be unable to right the wrongs of women, in our own case, in our own lifetime. We may also have to accept that we will pay a high price for taking responsibility for our own lives – if, for example, your refusal to accept your role leads you to end a relationship. On the other hand you will at least be living your life, rather than postponing it by compulsive eating.

Mrs White is a giant of a woman. She's been getting that way ever since she was first pregnant. She now has three small boys, the eldest about seven, the youngest about two. Every day her husband goes to work in the morning in a thoroughly conventional way, and she stays at home and looks after the children. She takes the eldest one to school and the middle one to nursery. Then she comes home with the little one and does housework until it's time to collect the middle one from nursery. They have lunch together. Then Mrs White clears up a bit while the little one has his nap. After that they go out so that she can get any shopping she needs on the way to picking up the big one from school. After they all get home Mrs White makes tea for the children, clears up again and makes some preparation for dinner for herself and her husband. Then it's time to get the children ready for bed. They've had their baths by the time Mr White comes back and he reads them their stories and puts them to bed while Mrs White finishes dinner for the adults. By the time they've eaten, cleared up, made some preparations for the next day and watched the news on television, it's time to go to bed. Both of them are really tired so they don't often make love; they just go straight off to sleep, because the youngest child will wake them pretty early in the morning.

Some women might like this way of living. Mrs White hates it – not that she knows it. She hides her fury and her guilt at her fury and her despair behind her enormous size, which she maintains by eating all day long. Her chores are punctuated by food. She feels guilty and miserable about the way she looks and the way she eats, and she wonders if it's her size that makes her husband not want to have sex any more. It's true that her fat can actually make it a bit awkward. Besides, she loves her children and her husband and wants to take care of them. She could do with spending some time thinking about her eating behaviour, couldn't she?

Stop and Think

How do you see your life as a woman? Women now, at least in theory, have far more choices than they have ever had. Education is readily available. Women can work in almost any occupation or profession. Women can choose whether they have children and whether they continue to work or how much they work. What are your ideas about how you would like your life to develop? What have you seen in the relationships of your parents and their generation that you find to admire and want to copy? What don't you like about the way that they conduct their relationships? What about your contemporaries? What do you see in the way that they have relationships that you admire and would like for yourself? What mistakes do you think that women of your age make in the way they organise their lives? Can you believe in your own power to choose to live your life in a way that fulfils your potential?

Chapter Five
The Difficulties of Growing Up

"On 9 January Margaret came from the ward to my room. . . . She was accompanied by a nurse, and, in spite of looking as though her skeleton-like body would be broken into pieces by the weight of the hospital blanket draped round her shoulders, she walked steadily and unaided. . . . I explained to her that treatment entailed her telling me any thoughts that came into her mind so that together we could try to understand why she was not wanting to eat. . . . She looked a little less pinched and cold and gradually moved her body so that she was curled up under her blanket in such a way that a picture of a baby feeding came immediately to my mind. . . . After a pause, in response to a slight movement in her body, I said I thought that she wanted to talk to me with her body as she had done to her mother before she could talk. . . . Up to this stage in her analysis her unconscious conflicts about growing up had been expressed mainly through her body in such things as gains and losses of weight."
— F. Tustin, *Autistic Barriers in Neurotic Patients*, 1986

Anorexia was the first of the eating disorders to be studied. Almost from the beginning it was thought that it was to do with problems of growing up into a woman. The most obvious features of anorexia are the delay or prevention of menstruation and the loss of weight. The loss of weight has sometimes been understood as a way for girls to get rid of the secondary sexual characteristics which include breasts and fat round the hips and bottom. When this understanding of weight loss has been put together with an ending of (or a failure to begin) periods, then it has sometimes been suggested that the point of anorexia, its function so far as the girl is concerned, is to keep her in a pre-sexual state both as far as her hormones and therefore her whole physical self are concerned, and also emotionally. It is a way of remaining pre-sexual emotionally. What follows, then, is the idea that the anorexic girl does not want to grow up, and particularly does not want to grow up sexually.

There are a good number of aspects to growing up, as well as sexual development – the capacity to separate from the family of origin, the capacity to be independent and to make decisions. These and other aspects will be discussed later as they relate both to anorexia and to compulsive eating, but this chapter focuses on developing sexuality as a part of growing up and the way in which it can be halted or reversed by anorexia. These ideas are also relevant to compulsive eating. The capacity to come to terms with our sexuality is both desirable and a mark of healthy adult development. For the vast majority of human beings, the capacity to form a long-term intimate, sexual relationship is the basis of adult contentment and creativity. There are, however, a number of different ways of handling our sexuality – among them the decision not to have sexual relationships at a certain time or perhaps at all. These decisions are perfectly valid, but cause less pain if they can be made from strength and not from fear. The disordered eater's rejection of sexuality is from fear, and it is this aspect that is discussed in this chapter.

Anna's anorexia seemed to have been precipitated by three events: her mother's hysterectomy; her best friend leaving the country perhaps for ever; and her own impending departure for college in London at the age of 18. Yet none of these things seemed to lie at the root of her illness and talking about them did not help. Gradually, with the support of her family and a circle of concerned helpers, she made a recovery over more than two years. When she was about to leave college after three years, she went to see the counsellor who had originally tried to help and talked about what she now understood about her illness. She said that she had been a lively and adventurous adolescent, exploring her world and experimenting with life, but in the face of major changes in her life she began to be afraid that she would not be able to control her adolescent experimentation, that she was in danger of 'going too far' and that she needed to put the brakes on hard. As she described it, she had as a result been standing still for three years.

Let us think a little more closely about the way in which she had been 'standing still'. It was clearly not in respect of her studies, since she had completed her course satisfactorily. It was in her social and sexual development that she had stood still. Anna was someone who had begun to have sexual relationships quite early. Yet for three years she had had no boyfriends and no sexual relationship. It was these feelings, these impulses and that behaviour which she had got rid of via her anorexia. In her case her self-starvation had been severe enough and prolonged enough to stop her menstruating. She had returned herself symbolically and literally to a pre-pubertal state where she was not troubled physically by the evidence of her sexual potential. The hormonal changes brought about by weight loss also remove sexual feelings. Even if that were not so, Anna was far too busy computing calories and worrying about what tiny amounts of food she would eat and when and where to be capable of noticing her sexual impulses. So here was a woman whose growing up had been negotiated well enough at puberty but who found it necessary to reverse that process temporarily at a moment of later crisis. By the time she came to the end of her course she felt able to resume her development as a person. Her need for time out was over.

Your Father's Daughter

One of the ideas some thinkers have had about anorexic girls who seem to have difficulty negotiating puberty and growing up is that for some of them growing out of being their father's daughter is too difficult. A young woman from an exceedingly prosperous and comfortable family had a very successful father. He was a distinguished architect and an attractive and charming man. Nancy was his adored daughter. She was pretty, clever, everything her father could wish for, and he was extremely proud of her. The pair had a very close, even intimate relationship, which at times excluded Nancy's mother. Nancy would spend whole evenings with her father in his study. They would talk and laugh and sometimes Nancy would sit on his knee. Only two things spoiled this idyllic pleasure. One was that Nancy's father could not bear her to go out with boys. Whenever a boy wanted to date her and came to the house, Nancy's father would make disparaging comments, so Nancy very soon felt the boy was no good after all. The other problem was that over the course of her adolescence Nancy had become steadily more anorexic. By 18 she had become bulimic and her life had focused on her eating disorder.

It is not very difficult to see what was going on in this family. In some sense Nancy had become her father's girlfriend (although there was no suggestion whatever of an overt sexual relationship between them). This had been achieved, at least in Nancy's eyes, at the expense of her mother. So you might say that in the competition for her father and his interest and attention, Nancy had won. Moreover, her father had played an energetic role in creating this situation. He had colluded in excluding Nancy's mother and he had also excluded male rivals from the scene by getting rid of any potential boyfriend for Nancy. The results were, however, disastrous for the father's marriage and for Nancy.

Nancy in a way had got what she wanted – the exclusive attention of her father – but she had paid a very high price for it. Her whole adolescent development had come to a halt and her conflict had become expressed in a serious eating disorder. She had managed to hold on to her childhood role of 'Daddy's girl', but only by sacrificing her healthy development into a woman. The pair of them were locked into a relationship that was not only long-time expired but also very destructive.

Some therapists working with anorexics have used methods of family therapy to help not only the sufferer but her whole family. Often it looks as though the meaning of a girl's reluctance to grow up is best understood in terms of the whole family's functioning. Certainly that seems likely in the case of Nancy's family. (Some information on families and anorexia is given in the resources in Chapter 12.)

Anna and Nancy are examples of women who found the transition to adult womanhood extremely difficult. The difficulty, however, can take the form of weight gain, rather than weight loss. Compulsive eating can delay the social and emotional development of an adolescent just as effectively as anorexia, although not in such a life-threatening way.

Jane's Story

Jane was in her early twenties when I met her. She came to see me not only because she was very seriously overweight but also because her size had had such a devastating effect on her self-esteem and confidence that she had dropped out of her college course and was living at home 'doing nothing', as she said. She had come to see me at her mother's insistence, a mother who was heartily sick of Jane's depression and inactivity. Being so overweight had done her no favours at all; she had been bullied at school and excluded from much of the social life of her classmates. She did still have a few friends but when they went on weekend shopping expeditions she could not take part in the pleasurable game of trying on clothes and looking for new outfits. Understandably, these expeditions were not very pleasant for her. She was also excluded by her size from trips to the cinema; the seats were just not big enough and the humiliation and discomfort of squeezing into them was more that she could bear. She had stuck with her A-level courses for quite a while but she found the field trips for geography exhausting and fitting behind the desks in the classroom was extremely awkward. Throughout this time Jane steadily continued to eat very large quantities of food and continued to gain weight.

It was abundantly clear from Jane's story that there were disadvantages attached to being so big. So why didn't she, as so many people constantly advised her, eat less and lose some weight. That became the question that we set out to answer between us. My understanding was that Jane would never put up with the torture of so much social exclusion and physical discomfort unless the food and her size had some value that was more important than those things. Why did she need the food and the weight? What needed to happen for her to give them up? We began our exploration by thinking about the history of Jane's weight gain. She had been a plump child, but not one who was seriously overweight. However, it seemed likely that even as a child she had learned the comforting value of food. Jane's parents owned a business that kept them very occupied and from an early age Jane had become accustomed to looking after herself. In attachment terms we could say that her experience had taught her that she needed to look after herself because nobody else would, and the way she had found of doing it was via packets of crisps and bags of sweets. You could say then that Jane had already learned, well before she became a teenager, that food can make you feel better.

When Jane was ten an incident occurred that might have frightened any child of her age: a man exposed himself to her when she was coming home through the park from school. Had Jane's parents been available for her to run home to and tell how frightened and confused this made her feel, all might have been well. But they were at work and in any case she had not developed the habit of turning to them in time of need; she turned to food instead. That experience was compounded by some bullying from a group of boys at the senior school she went to when she was 11. As a new girl in a strange environment, she was vulnerable to much older boys who ambushed her and threatened to take her knickers off and see what she looked like. When Jane started to cry the boys, who were probably careless rather than malicious, got scared themselves and said they were only joking and let her go. As in the experience a year previously, she didn't go home and blurt out how very upset and frightened she was, but instead again turned to food. This second trauma was ongoing, because of course she saw those boys at school most days and still said nothing. By the time she was 13 she weighed 13 stone and had begun her career as the fat girl who doesn't interest the boys.

So what could be done about all this and how could Jane's feelings that boys were cruel and nasty change? Just telling the story and making some sense of her very rapid weight gain between the ages of 10 and 13, and continued weight gain since, made Jane feel a hundred times better. She might not like her eating behaviour and size, but at least it made sense to her as a means of protection and survival. So she could let go of the idea that she was just greedy or lazy or stupid or any of the other insults that she regularly had to hear. She had been looking after herself as well as she knew how, in very difficult circumstances. This understanding also enabled her to start to do things a bit differently.

She began by talking to her parents. They were not bad or neglectful or unsympathetic people, far from it. They were hard-working, goodhearted people who had been doing what they thought best to support themselves and Jane. They had been puzzled and upset for ten years by Jane's weight gain and had done their best, by paying for exercise classes and diet clubs, to help her deal with the problem. It had never crossed their minds that there might be any underlying problem and they saw Jane's habit of keeping things to herself as her way of managing. They made no connection between her overeating and her emotional state – and why should they since nowhere in all the professional advice they sought had anyone suggested there might be a psychological or emotional meaning to Jane's weight.

When Jane began to tell them how lonely she had been when they were out at work and how unhappy, and how she now realised that she had dealt with those feelings by eating, her parents were very upset. They were particularly distressed to realise that they had never noticed Jane's self-soothing with sweets, cakes and crisps. They had seen themselves as trying their upmost to get back home to Jane and had thought that providing her with goodies would make the waiting more bearable. They were right, it had. But they had no clue as to how much she had missed them and how much she had learned that habit of soothing herself with food. Even though none of this could be undone, the conversations, which took place over several weeks, started a habit of communication within the family that was new and, although uncomfortable to begin with, made them feel closer. After some time Jane felt brave enough to tell them about the incidents in the past: the man who had exposed himself and the boys who had ambushed her. This time her parents were really shocked, not just by the stories themselves but more by the realisation of what Jane had kept to herself. Her father was all for identifying the boys and reporting them to the police, but Jane felt no useful purpose would be served by that. Instead she told her parents she wanted to change the way she managed her life. She wanted to be able to talk to them much more and be more open about what went on with her. Now remember that Jane was 21 – and getting close to your parents isn't something most 21-year-olds want to do – but Jane had never practised sharing her feelings. She was trying to continue with her parents the new ways of relating that she had started to learn in counselling. She had told me the story and learned that perhaps some people can be trusted and will respond to emotional need. By talking to her parents she was exploring whether she could do that with her family.

In this process Jane began to lose weight, not by going on a diet but by having a much clearer idea of when she might be eating to soothe herself, and in those situations becoming much more aware of her feelings and responses. She learned many new strategies for managing her feelings. She learned how to talk to herself in a soothing way; she developed soothing words, phrases and images that she could use in an emergency; she learned to use music and reading and taking care of herself with manicures and hairdos. So of course she used food less and so lost weight. As she lost weight she began to integrate better with her contemporaries and to learn from them the lessons she had missed while she was sitting at home alone. None of this happened quickly. It took three years before Jane was a weight that she found acceptable, but by then she had also got herself a qualification and then a job. She had started to go out with boys, and although she had suffered the usual heartache of relationships, she was no longer paralysingly afraid.

Stop and Think

Although talking to yourself kindly and compassionately and finding other people who will help and support you are, in my view, the best ways of managing our lives, we all have a portfolio of strategies for soothing ourselves. Think about what you use or could use, which is not harmful to you and make a list to remind yourself. I'm thinking about things such as listening to music, getting some exercise, playing with the dog/cat, reading, watching television, pursuing a hobby, gardening, dancing, etc.

Jade's Story

Jade was 15 years old when she went to see the school counsellor. She would probably never have asked for help herself, but her head of year had noticed her frequent absences from school and had heard repeated stories that she was being bullied. The bullies had been confronted and what emerged was that Jade was being called a lesbian. There were graffiti around the school about her and all sorts of minor but horrible encounters had made her feel really persecuted. Most of this came from other girls – Jade's possessions were stolen or damaged; there were sly physical attacks on her, hair pulling, pushing, kicks in the ankles as she walked past other girls. Over the same time Jade had put on a great deal of weight, so she was also being called names about her size. Not surprisingly, she was extremely unhappy.

It took some time for this story to emerge, but what was clear almost from the first session was that Jade was self-harming and felt suicidal. It was urgent that the reason behind all this distress was quickly understood and managed. What followed was Jade's terrible anxiety and uncertainty about her sexuality. Was she a lesbian, as everyone else seemed to think? It was true that she wasn't very interested in boys, but it was also true that she found the company of many of her female classmates very uninteresting. She felt as if there was no place for her. She had not even attempted to talk to her parents. Her father had a military background and often talked in very disparaging ways about homosexuality. Her mother had once said in Jade's hearing that she didn't believe there was such a thing as female homosexuality. It was not surprising that Jade felt there was little likelihood of being understood at home. She felt utterly isolated and rejected. In that situation it was hardly surprising that she had turned to food. At least bars of chocolate did not attack and abuse her.

In this situation the last thing that Jade needed was pressure to lose weight. Food was how she was managing; she needed that strategy until she could find a better way to cope. The fundamental task for Jade was to develop a more compassionate and accepting attitude towards herself within which she could start to explore how she felt about sex with males or females, how her sexuality had developed up to this point, what it would mean for her to be heterosexual or homosexual. Where she found herself was in a culture at school and at home where homosexuality was thought to be so alien and so unacceptable that it was extremely difficult for her even to begin to think about these issues. The counsellor's calm, accepting and interested attitude gradually created a trusting relationship within which Jade did start to think about these issues. The counsellor also pointed her in the direction of books that discussed teenage sexuality and websites where she could read what other people thought, and hear about their struggles and uncertainties[1]. All this created a bit of space for Jade. She felt more confident that she was allowed to have her questions and her complicated feelings. The school's robust attitude to the bullying helped. The school peer support system began to work in her favour and Jade's more open acknowledgement that, yes, maybe she was a lesbian but she didn't really know, won her the respect of at least some of her tormentors. She was able to attend school regularly and concentrate on her classes and homework, so that she could get the exam results that would enable her to continue her education. By the time Jade went into the sixth form she had found a circle of friends and the bad days were over. That, of course, was not the end of the story, but it was the end of the time when Jade needed to take care of herself with food. She no longer binged and slowly, without really trying, she lost weight. At that point she could also let go of the counselling, which had been a lifesaver for her for a whole year. She had learned that it was possible to find people who liked and respected her and who listened with interest to what she had to say. That experience taught her to respect herself more and to believe in her own value and importance.

Daisy's Story

Daisy was someone who had been anorexic in her mid-teens. She had one brother two years older. Her parents had had a struggle to make a living and in the process the children had suffered some emotional neglect. Probably as a result of this, the two children had sought comfort from each other and there had been a physical relationship between them for some years while they were both pre-pubertal.

This had caused Daisy a very difficult mixture of feelings of pleasure and guilt. This in itself would have made puberty difficult, but the class expectations of Daisy as an adolescent were that she would leave school, marry young and begin to have children soon after. The model of the life that awaited her, as her mother's daughter, was one of domesticity and isolation while her husband went out to work. Daisy's father had a business that he greatly enjoyed running, evidently more than he enjoyed being at home with his wife and family since as a child Daisy saw little of him. Daisy saw her mother as weak, passive and devalued, but also vulnerable. When her parents argued, in Daisy's perception the quarrels were always brought to an end by her father saying to her mother, 'Well, if you don't like it, you know what you can do. You can pack your bags.'

So, then, there was difficult early sexual experience for Daisy to deal with. There was a social role that for her was uninviting for a number of reasons, but there was also something else. The father of one of Daisy's friends had exposed himself to her and shown her pornographic magazines. This had been frightening for Daisy, then about 12 or 13 years old, so frightening and so guilt-provoking that she told no one. She felt herself in some way to blame. All of this she might still have coped with, and indeed did for a while in that she began to menstruate and to be interested in boys. However, at 15 she was seduced by a much older man. This was finally more than she could deal with and she became anorexic.

Daisy had grown up in an environment where having sexual wishes and feelings carried excitement, but also too much guilt and fear. As she got older those wishes and feelings became stronger. She got rid of her feelings, her wishes, her sexuality, even her memories for a time, in the wholehearted pursuit of emaciation. She had felt there was no one who could help her deal with her sexuality, no one she could talk to about her fears and her guilt. Now that she was anorexic she made absolutely sure that she did get the attention she needed.

However, it was of course the wrong kind of attention. Instead of the understanding and the holding that she needed, she provoked irritation and anger. She came from a family with very conventional eating behaviour. They were a meat and two-veg. sort of family for whom Sunday dinner was an important social occasion. Daisy's wish to be a vegetarian, her refusal to eat what her mother cooked, her sitting and not eating and not contributing at family mealtimes – all of it provoked concern, then anger, then despair. Daisy, of course, had no idea what the problem was. I say 'of course' because if she had been able to know what was bothering her, she might not have needed to be anorexic.

Then even more difficult times began because Daisy had started to lose the ability simply to go on starving herself and began to maintain her low weight by bingeing, vomiting or purging. The control Daisy had managed to maintain up to that point was broken and the whole of her life began to be as chaotic as her new eating behaviour. Her sexual appetite, as if to convince her that all of her fears about herself were true, became frantic and desperate. At the same time the bit of her that was still a terrified child was visible from time to time when she became afraid to be left alone in her boyfriend's flat.

In all of this horror there were two points of stability. One was Daisy's parents. Despite their anger and their incomprehension, they held on. They maintained contact with her; they allowed her to come home whenever she wanted to, despite the fact that such visits were often very uncomfortable for everyone. In fact they loved their daughter as well as they knew how. The second point of consistency was Daisy's dancing. During all the painful years of her adolescence and early twenties she was training as a dancer and then teaching dance, both choreography and performance. It would not be true to say that this had been easy. There had been many moments of anguish and despair, but at the same time dancing gave Daisy some self-respect. At least she was working and that helped her to hold on to some sense of her own value.

Very slowly she began to get better. She found herself some therapy and courageously began to look at what had been going on with her. Her eating difficulties did not go away at once or easily. It seemed as though when Daisy felt again the old despair and distress about her sexuality, she would retreat into her eating disorders for a day or a few days or a week. But Daisy had in fact learned a great deal and it was not all that long before she was able to deal with her feelings more directly and even believe that she was not wrong or bad for wanting a sexual relationship with a man.

One of the ways of keeping an eating disorder at hand, ready for such emotional crises, is to belong to a profession where thinness is required. There are many dancers with eating disorders and even more whose eating is disordered and they live in a culture where close attention to weight and shape is the norm. The same could be said of a number of other ways of life – that of a model, for example, or a gymnast. In each of these activities a high value is placed on extreme thinness and a pre-pubertal unwomanly shape. Dancing in particular and the dance world have often been accused of creating anorexia, but perhaps the influence is in fact the other way round – that people who feel as if at any moment they might need their eating disorder gravitate towards an environment where their obsessiveness is less noticeable, more permissible.

Stop and Think

How relevant to you are the ideas in this chapter? Sex and sexuality are difficult and complicated for most people – is it possible that you manage your anxieties about these issues by using food?

Think about how you learned about sex – do you feel that experience was helpful and enjoyable or were your early realisations about sex difficult and problematic?

Are you someone who has had traumatic experience of sex – for instance, rape, incest, sexual abuse? Have these experiences contributed to or triggered your disordered eating?

Have you found it difficult to come to terms with your sexuality? Might that be the reason for you using food the way you do?

There are, however, many of us who from time to time retreat into anorexic episodes in relation to our difficulties with our sexuality. Difficulties in our relationships, or even the prospect of a relationship (and therefore of sexual feelings and needs) can trigger off these times. The anguish of starving, or of bingeing and starving, is a hard way to deal with difficulties. These ways of coping do nothing to help us deal with our underlying difficulties. They keep us stuck, fixed, at the same place in our development. They keep us from growing as people. We all have and we all need ways of coping, but to try and deal with the painfulness of being a sexual woman by torturing and hurting our bodies must surely be something we need to leave behind.

Chapter Six
At Least I'll Control
What I Put in My Mouth

"An image came to her, that she was like a sparrow in a golden cage, too plain and simple for the luxuries of her home, but also deprived of the freedom of doing what she truly wanted to do. Until then she had spoken only about the superior features of her background; now she began to speak about the ordeal, the restrictions and obligations of growing up in a wealthy home."

— Hilde Bruch *The Golden Cage: The Enigma of Anorexia Nervosa*, 2001

Felicity's Story

There is a kind of family, usually white, usually prosperous middle class, which is intensely protective of its children, especially its girl children. Let me describe such a family. Felicity is in her late teens and very, very thin. She has an exceedingly slender and fragile neck which makes her look frail and vulnerable. She comes from a family where her father is a successful businessman. She has one sister who is two years older and a mother who, as long as Felicity can remember, has stayed at home and spent all her time and energy on looking after her family. They have a lovely new house and it is beautifully clean and well tended. Since she was born Felicity has been taken care of very well. She has always been able to have pretty much what she wants materially – in fact it has been her parents' pleasure to provide it for her. Nowadays she has some nice clothes, much nicer than most of her contemporaries, but she looks after them much more carefully than they do theirs anyway, and makes sure that they are clean and ironed. Her mother does most of that for her.

One of the ways in which Felicity's mother has tried to take the best possible care of her is in providing food. When Felicity was a schoolgirl her mother was always there in the afternoon after school with something to eat to carry her over until dinnertime. Whenever she goes anywhere her mother provides her with a beautifully thought out and put together packed lunch, and nowadays whenever she gets home from work there is a meal waiting for her.

This business of food is difficult for Felicity and has been for quite a long time. When she was a schoolgirl she used sometimes to tell her mother that she didn't need to be there every day. She, Felicity, was old enough to take care of herself; wasn't there something that her mother wanted to do for herself? But her mother said no, she didn't mind being there when Felicity came home, and anyway she felt it was her duty. She wouldn't feel at all easy about Felicity coming home to an empty house.

Over the last few years Felicity has become very thin indeed, partly because she turns down a lot of what her mother offers her. Of course this makes her mother very anxious and she presses food on Felicity, but that only makes her even more determined not to accept it. She feels that her mother wants her to eat more than she should. In any case, these days Felicity does a lot of dancing and needs to be thin to go on with that.

It seems clear that Felicity is using food and her capacity to refuse to eat her mother's food as a way of trying to separate herself from an intensely close, concerned and protective family. Her big sister is a bit tougher than Felicity in some ways. When she was growing up she had rows and disagreements with her parents. This won her sister her freedom and independence, so that she has now gone off to university in another city and created a life and circle of friends of her own. Felicity was frightened by these rows and saw how much they upset her parents. Besides she feels she was never allowed to get angry or to answer back and she doesn't really know how to defy them.

This is not to say that Felicity hasn't tried to strike out a bit on her own. She has, but it is difficult because her parents want to do everything for her. When she does try to do something for herself it never seems to work out, or at least never as well as when her parents do it for her. Take, for instance, the first time she decided to move out of home and get a place for herself. She was determined to do it on her own. She looked in the newspapers and tried to team up with other people to get a place, but it kept falling through. Finally, she decided to go it on her own and use a flat agency. The agency found her a flat and charged her a huge fee. However, the flat was really pretty horrible, dirty and not in a very good part of town. Within a few weeks Felicity decided it wouldn't do. This incident left her with a tremendous sense of failure. When she had summoned up all her courage (and it had taken a lot) to try and move out of home, she had made a mess of it.

It makes it more complicated that with part of her Felicity doesn't in the least want to separate from her parents. In some ways their endless concern is irritating. She wishes they wouldn't phone her every day, or at least wait for her to phone them. But on the other hand her own home is beautifully clean, whereas the shared areas of the flat where she now lives are dirty. Besides, everything is so convenient and so ready to hand in her parents' home.

When she doesn't know what she really wants in all these other areas Felicity finds some comfort in at least taking control over what she puts into her mouth. She is very health conscious and a vegetarian, and there are many things she would not dream of eating. When so much of the rest of her life feels unsatisfactory, Felicity can at least create one corner where it feels as if she is in charge.

But she is not very much in charge, even in this corner, as she knows all too well. She doesn't know when she's hungry or what she wants to eat, or how much is a good amount to eat, any more than she knows what she wants in other directions. She has had very little practice in knowing what she wants – even whether she wants juice or milk, or a whole or half glass. Her mother made those choices and decisions. But she has had a lot of practice in knowing what other people think she should have. As far as the anorexia goes, she has made up a lot of rules about what she will and won't eat, and that makes her feel more as if she knows what she wants. But of course it's a very difficult system to maintain and takes up a lot of energy.

As far as Felicity is concerned, her anorexic behaviour seems to symbolise two things. One is her conflict about whether she does or does not want to try and be separate from her parents. Of course, practically speaking, while she is so thin there is no way that they are going to relax their hold. They don't think she looks after herself properly and they are right, although they have no real idea of how badly she does. This holding on, that she has ensured will continue, symbolises the side of her that finds the idea of separation utterly terrifying and feels that 'living her own life' is something she is quite incapable of doing.

The other part of the story, though, is the way Felicity feels that her life depends on the degree to which she can hold her mother's smothering love at arm's length. When she rejects her mother's food (and then the food her own internal mother tempts her to eat) she is rejecting a love that feels to her as if it traps her in a state of permanent dependency. With part of her she wants above all else not to be dependent. Dependency feels infinitely dangerous. She is denying her need for food/love, keeping it out.

If Felicity wanted either of these things alone – dependence or independence – things would be much simpler. But she has tremendous conflict inside her, not only in her body. We might also add that Felicity's mother is perhaps not a very encouraging model for Felicity. Her mother is practically and emotionally totally dependent on Felicity's father, yet within that dependency her function is to look after everybody else; that is what her life is about. How does Felicity dare to grow up and be separate? How does she dare not to?

But remember, Felicity's older sister has managed these difficulties rather well and her example is intensely important. Slowly Felicity begins to be able to feel and to voice some of her conflicts and, in the process, her eating problems begin to resolve. It involves a change for her parents too because they have to learn how to let their child grow up and therefore how to see themselves differently. Felicity's mother particularly has invested a great deal in her mothering. Can she find a way of developing herself now that her children are grown up, and will her husband also be able to adjust to the changes in his wife's role as well as in his own? They both find it painful that Felicity now tries to express to them the ways in which she feels they have failed her. They did love her and they do love her and they did what they did with the best will in the world.

There are lots of hopeful features about Felicity's life, not the least the fact that her anorexia has never taken over her life the way it can do. She works and she has been able to let herself know enough about her mixed feelings about growing up, about separation and independence, above all about her mother, so that she has not had to express everything through her body. As she can feel and explore these difficult areas more, there is a very good chance that she will be able to make a complete recovery.

Stop and Think

Where do you think you are in relation to this issue of separation and independence? Are you trapped in a conflict of wanting to strike out on your own and being afraid to do so? Are you worried about the effect on your mother (or father) of you taking charge of your own life? Could it be that your eating behaviour is the only way you have yet found to express that dilemma?

Elisabeth's Story

In a way Felicity's situation and her way of dealing with it are fairly easy to understand. Elisabeth's story is much more complicated. She too comes from a prosperous, conventional, middle-class household. Her father, like Felicity's, began with very little. He has worked hard for his success and is proud of his ability to provide generously for the material needs of his wife and two children – Elisabeth and a boy two years older. Her mother now works as a teacher, but for a lot of her children's childhood she stayed at home because she wanted to provide a secure base for them. She has been intensely protective of Elisabeth who remembers her childhood as a time of never being allowed to do anything for herself, or on her own.

Until puberty all went reasonably well, although Elisabeth now thinks that her mother's anxieties about what 'other people' would think made spontaneity and freedom in behaviour and relationships very difficult. But when Elisabeth reached puberty she began to be intensely pressured by the expectations of her parents. Her mother was apparently afraid of Elisabeth's approaching womanhood and did her best to deny its existence. For example, she would not allow Elisabeth to buy a bra when she felt she needed to. She herself had only ever had one boyfriend, Elisabeth's father, whom she had met at 16, fallen in love with and married some years later. This model was held up to Elisabeth as the one that was desirable. Her daughter's wishes to explore and experiment with friendships with boys were met with fear and resistance. At the same time Elisabeth's father had strong academic ambitions for his daughter. He wanted her to go to Oxford (as he himself had not done) and felt that a social life was simply a distraction from this more serious aim.

It took Elisabeth until she was 17 to assert herself in the face of these parental expectations, but at that point she insisted on having more of a social life and at the same time continued with studying for A Levels. Still, looking back at it, she feels that even then there were signs that she was dealing with her difficulties by the use of food. She remembers that she was unable to study unless she was eating sweets at the same time. Perhaps we can understand this sweet eating as a way of dealing with her anxiety about whether her academic and social ambitions could be reconciled: can clever girls be sexy? Marilyn Lawrence[1] has written about the way that 'education' can pose hideous problems for clever girls who have grown up in a world where many men are still threatened by clever, educated women. Evidently men often marry women younger and less educated than themselves. It is easy to see what kind of a tight corner Elisabeth might be getting herself into, and how hard it was likely to be for her to know what she wanted for herself.

She was managing not too badly and might have survived these conflicts without a lot of anguish, but sadly she had one pressure too many to deal with. She had left school and won a place at a university – not Oxford – when her boyfriend was killed in a car accident. This was doubly traumatic for Elisabeth since after a series of relationships in which she had been careful not to get too involved, she had allowed herself to become very dependent on this particular young man. Her first year at university was a year of anorexia which resulted in her dropping out.

In some ways Elisabeth's anorexia had much in common with Felicity's. Like Felicity, Elisabeth's anorexia expressed both her anguish about dependency and her need to reject the stifling kind of love that her parents seemed to offer, and to take control of her life, but at the same time showing to all the world by her thinness her desperate need for care and concern. Elisabeth had conformed to her father's wish that she should go to university, while at the same time knowing in some corner of her mind that it was not for her. Yet it was impossible for her to confront and oppose her father. Her anorexia was in part a translation into physical terms of her need to defy him. Of course she did not know that. If she had known it, she might not have needed to do it. Her anorexia achieved the desired result very effectively – she dropped out of university. By the time she decided on a different path to follow, her father was so anxious about her that he was glad to go along with whatever Elisabeth wanted to do.

However, Elisabeth's anorexia was more complex than that. In part it was to assert some control over her life by defying her father, but it was also to deny and keep at arm's length the sexual and emotional needs that had allowed her to make a relationship with a man in which she was dependent. Her dependency as a child had resulted in the stunting of her necessary and ordinary development towards independence and separation. She both craved and was terrified of her dependency needs. You could say that her attachment experience had left her without confidence in her own resources. When she finally permitted herself to experience dependency with a boy, he was then killed. What Elisabeth learned from this was once again that dependency was too dangerous. Her anorexia said 'I have no needs', but her body shape said 'My needs are not being met.'

To summarise briefly, there appears to be a sort of family which stifles the growth towards independence and separation of its girl children (and more rarely its boys) by over-protectiveness, by intrusiveness, by not allowing those daughters enough room to develop. Sometimes those girls will rebel against that state of affairs by anorexia. In these cases anorexics can be seen both as rejecting what will otherwise stifle, and as a way of taking control of a small part of their lives (but in the end all of their lives). In some ways anorexia is a deafening 'NO', shouted by someone who has never learned to speak.

The Silent Signals

It is this 'NO' that is the most obvious part of the illness. Anyone who has ever dealt with anorexics can testify to what a deafening shout it is, and how powerful it is in getting other people to co-operate and obey. It is so frustrating and frightening for other people that it can provoke reactions just as violent. Perhaps that is why people treating anorexics are quite often cruel. The massive rejection is not easy to bear.

However, it is very important to remember that the message given by the anorexic is after all not that clear. We must also remember that this scream 'NO' is not the only message that an anorexic is giving (or that you are giving in your anorexic episodes). What must not be forgotten is that weight loss and not eating are also public statements of something very different: of need, of dependency, of fragility. The problem for an anorexic, or indeed for anyone with eating disorders, is that she is caught in a very tight corner. With one part of us we want one thing and want it desperately, but with another we want something quite different, and want that with equal passion. The struggle, the battle, gets fought out for those of us with disordered eating over food.

The 'NO' of the anorexic produces responses in other people which activate their 'yes'. They need other people to say 'yes' for them. Sometimes the 'yes' of other people ('I want you to eat something; you're not eating enough; you're getting terribly thin; I'm worried about you not eating') is used in part by an anorexic as a way of holding on to her 'NO' (if you say 'yes' I'll say 'NO') and becomes part of the meaning of the anorexia. The struggle between yes and no becomes part of the struggle for power, for control, in a woman's life. However, even quite short-lived and sub-clinical anorexia is also very frightening, as well as being exciting and defiant. The anorexic needs to know that even if she will not for the moment say 'yes', there are other people who will say 'yes' for her.

In the end, of course, no one can say 'yes' for us if we will not find the 'yes' in ourselves. Doctors, hospitals, parents will go to all sorts of extreme lengths to say 'yes' for us – forced feeding, intravenous drips, behavioural programming, and so on. However, we all have the power to say 'no' to life, to love, to food. If in the end we decide that this 'NO' is all we can say, then we can do that. We can die, as so sadly some women do, or as tragically, we can destroy our lives with a constant preoccupation with food, weight and size. This life, this now, is all we have. It seems so sad to throw it away.

Fortunately, however, there are comparatively few ano-rexics who are so desperate. What many do instead is to fight out that yes and no in their bodies, using food to do it with – which is exactly what happened with Elisabeth. She had a year of what might be called straightforward anorexia. She didn't eat very much and what she ate she consumed secretly and on her own. She lost a great deal of weight and became a recluse, holed up in her room in a university hall of residence, not working, not going to classes. Finally, someone noticed and intervened. She was found medical and psychological help and in the course of about six months made at least a partial recovery.

So far, so good. Elisabeth's anorexia had actually been quite effective in some ways. Her fight to control her life had been won in some areas – she was out of university and exploring other educational possibilities. However, this was only one element of Elisabeth's anorexia. Her eating disorder was also a response to her boyfriend's death and was to do with her difficulties with dependency and intimacy. Her anorexia was then partly to do with a rejection of these things, and therefore also a rejection of sexuality. Compared to the complexity and painfulness of all this, her victory over her father was not very much. She had abolished her dependency needs; she had said a resounding 'NO' to intimacy, but that left her isolated and with very painful needs for someone else. After all, you will remember that Elisabeth had been brought up in a family where there had been very little opportunity for her development as a separate, independent human being. With part of her she was terrified by her isolation and found it difficult and painful being on her own.

In a person without the need to translate these conflicts into eating behaviour they might have emerged in the form of a series of intense relationships, made and broken off – a pattern of can't do with it, can't do without it. In fact what Elisabeth did was to enter into an exceedingly dependent relationship with a man, but a man who had very difficult and deprived beginnings and was himself struggling with his dependency needs. He could not meet her needs in any very creative way because he had the same difficulties to confront. So Elisabeth found herself addicted to someone who couldn't really help her, but who needed her desperately and so constantly reinforced her dependency on him.

Elisabeth did not analyse any of this then. She couldn't. So far as she knew she was desperately in love. Then she began vomiting up her food. It was as if she enacted with her body what she could not recognise in her relationship. She needed and wanted closeness, sex, intimacy. More than that, with a bit of her she wanted to be a baby, a tiny child, looked after every minute of the day, attended to in every little detail, never left alone, held, cuddled, caressed and protected. So she wanted to eat, to take in, to be nourished, fed, sustained by good food. But at the same time she wanted to be her own woman, dependent on no one, alone, on her own, doing her own thing, not stifled by someone else's presence. Closeness, sex, another person's demands on her produced rage, hate and panic. So she got rid of what she had put inside her. She forced out of her body those good things that she had just put inside it. They had become bad, poisoning, hurtful to her. Not that she said that to herself. What she said was that she had eaten too much and that she was a greedy pig and would get fat and ugly, so she had better get rid of it.

It is clear that so far as food was concerned Elisabeth was operating in terms of all or nothing. Either she binged or she starved, feasted or fasted. If she ate anything she would eat too much. Yet this had its emotional aspect too. Either she was totally independent, isolated, without relationships, or she was engulfed, smothered. Either extreme had its good points and its bad. The ferocity of the conflict produced her bulimia, the violent and rapid swing between 'yes' and 'no'.

There could be no resolution to this horrible dilemma until Elisabeth could believe that there was more possible in relationships than these violent extremes. Gradually she began to talk to her parents and to express some of what she felt about the past. Slowly the three of them began to work out a way of relating in which Elisabeth no longer treated them either as the enemy or as a bottomless well of resources on which she could draw as she liked. In their turn they began to recognise that their daughter was no longer a child, but a capable and talented young woman with the ability to make decisions about her life. This modification was a great relief to both sides.

This exploration of the alternatives to the extremes of 'yes' and 'no' continued as Elisabeth found a grandmother figure with whom she could discover that there could be care and concern without stifling, and a boyfriend who had sorted out some of his dependency needs and knew how to be separate without being rejecting and how to be intimate without being smothering. As all this went on, Elisabeth's eating disorder began to be less tormenting, less preoccupying. Gradually she began to need that way of expressing herself much less often. The omens for her recovery and development look reasonably good.

Stop and Think

When you think about your own life, how good are you at finding the middle way between solitude and intimacy? Are you frightened of being taken over by another person so that you feel stifled and controlled, and if you look back to your family was that part of your experience growing up? How about solitude, does being on your own and not in a relationship feel terrifying? Does solitude make it very difficult for you to know what you want or even who you are?

What experience have you had of a relationship that seems to you to manage the conflict between intimacy and solitude? Have you seen couples interacting who seem to know how to manage that conflict? Do you have relationships with friends, or within your family, where you manage better? Can you use those examples as a way to figure out how a relationship can be supportive without being stifling and mutually dependent, rather than demanding one person's surrender?

Chapter Seven
Mothers and Daughters

"We are a generation who, with every act of self-assertion as women, with every movement into self-development and fulfilment, call into question the values by which our mothers have tried to live."

— Kim Chernin, *The Hungry Self*, 1994

Over the past 50 years those who are concerned with the effect early experience has on later life have increasingly turned to look at the part the mother has played, and away from the role of the father. This has not always had very creative results. Fathers and their influence have been ignored while at the same time 'bad' mothers have been blamed for all that is unsatisfactory. Feminists are to be thanked for the enormous amount of work they have done on mother–daughter relationships and for giving us a vocabulary and a way of thinking that can be extremely useful in helping us to reflect upon what goes on between mothers and daughters. This chapter owes a lot to their work, especially to Susie Orbach and Louise Eichenbaum.[1] This chapter also owes a lot to Kim Chernin.[2] She has been particularly interested in the connection between the mother–daughter relationship and eating disorders.

Monica's Story

Monica had a very difficult, troubled beginning to her life. She had to grow up much too quickly and had played a role in her family far beyond her emotional capacity. For her the complication lay in the fact that her father had divorced her mother, leaving her penniless and looking after a handicapped son who would never be able to live alone. Monica had plenty of rage and plenty of unmet need to deal with in relation to her mother, but she also saw that her mother was herself extremely hungry and empty and that her life was very unhappy. How could Monica go off and be happy, contented and successful when her mother was so unhappy and deprived? I think it is not exaggerating to say (as Monica eventually said herself) that she was determined not to be happy. The way she chose to be unhappy (or one of the ways) was to have an eating disorder. It prevented her from being successful in her work because it led to absences; it got in the way of her relationship with her boyfriend because it could be so preoccupying; it prevented her from enjoying her appearance (and she was beautiful) because it made her look and feel terrible; it stopped any possibility that she might think well of herself because she so hated and despised herself for misusing food.

Now what is the sense in an unhappy mother's misery being equalled by the unhappiness of her daughter? How will that help or make things better? In ordinary everyday logic, of course, it will not, but at one level it made good sense to Monica. To her being happy and successful felt like an attack on her mother, felt like abandoning her, even killing her. Her answer to this dilemma was that she would be unsuccessful and she used her eating disorder to make her so. She was identifying with her mother.

How could this shift or change? What could get Monica out of this dilemma? Part of what was going on, and it is not uncommon in women who have had to grow up too quickly, was that Monica was confused between the adult part of her which could see her mother's need and the child part of her which had always known about it and grown up quickly in order to try to look after it. On a rational adult basis it was true that Monica's mother was not in a very good situation. She was miserable, short of money and trapped by the needs of her handicapped child. On the other hand, the best way for Monica to help her, again on a rational basis, might well have been for her to be as successful as possible so that she would have some money to give to her mother. As to her mother's misery, Monica knew rationally that her mother had always been miserable, that she, Monica, had never been able to help her mother to be happy in the past and that she was unlikely to be able to do so now. Monica would do very well if she sorted out her own problems and miseries. She could not save her mother's soul for her, although it was sad that this was so.

It seemed that Monica was much more in touch with the part of her that perceived her mother's situation with the eye of the small child, catapulted too soon into adult responsibilities. She felt that she was being asked to take care of her mother's needs (and historically she probably was). What the child part of her could not see then and could not see now was that those demands were inappropriate and impossible. Neither as a child nor as an adult was it possible for her to make her mother happy. None of us can take responsibility for another person's happiness. Our happiness is our own responsibility.

Caroline's Story

Caroline's mother had come to Britain from abroad as a young woman and had never reconciled herself to the loss of her own mother and exile from her native land. She was a miserably depressed woman and again Caroline grew up far too quickly in her attempt to take care of her mother. Caroline's anger with her mother was, however, much more obvious than Monica's. At 16 she left home for good, deaf to her father's advice that she should do A Levels. She desperately wanted to be out of an environment in which her mother seemed to demand everything and give nothing. She was furious with her mother for being such a victim.

However, although Caroline's anger had blasted her out of her family home, it could not blast her mother out of her head. Caroline worried a lot about her, desperately wanted to make her happy, felt terribly guilty about abandoning her. Again, like Monica, she felt she must not be happy and successful herself. Her preoccupation with food made sure that she never felt confident about herself, prevented her from having boyfriends, reduced her capacity to work effectively and gave her reason to hate and despise herself.

For both of these women there was a lot of hate and anger in the way they treated themselves. This is often the case for food misusers; the hate and anger that they are directing against themselves is what they feel for other people. Both Monica and Caroline were in a rage with their mothers as well as identifying with them in their pain, but neither of them could acknowledge that fact. After all, how could these two women be angry with mothers so pathetic and so miserable? Instead they violently attacked themselves.

In a way, however, they were also attempting to fill the hole inside themselves left by mothering that had not been good enough. They were trying to respond to needs within themselves that had never been recognised or met. In reality neither of them had been able during their growing up to express the hate and anger that we all have in a good situation, let alone in a bad one. Their mothers gave them no help in dealing with these feelings and so they both learned not to know about them and to translate them into the language of food.

Both of them had a lot of work to do thinking about their mothers. For Monica that had to be done with me. Her mother was simply not capable of talking about what had gone on between her and Monica. Caroline was able to work quite a lot with her mother. There was a lot of shouting and crying, but it ended up with Caroline having a much better relationship with her mother and much less of a problem with food. What they had both missed was a mother who could attend to their child needs or, to put it another way, to whom they could have a secure attachment. Neither of them could rely on their mother to respond to their emotional need and so both had become 'young carers', but caring for their mothers emotionally rather than physically. Unfortunately, this strategy left them without the resources to meet their own needs. Because they had not been shown how to look after themselves, they were left with an emptiness that they both attempted to deal with via a preoccupation with food. This original deficit could not be mended. There was no way that those mothers could now make up for what had been lacking. However, human beings are remarkably capable of healing and mending. Both Monica and Caroline could understand what they had missed and in different ways come to terms with those circumstances. They could both also learn how to use first me and then other people to experience the kind of concern and care that we all need and which can teach us how to care for ourselves.

Stop and Think
- Would you say you were a young carer?
- Do you catch yourself wondering how your mother will manage without you?
- Do you feel as if you have to take care of her?
- Do you think that that role has made it hard for you to look after yourself appropriately?
- Is that why you use food?

Competition between Mothers and Daughters

There are other ways, however, in which women find the relationship with their mothers so difficult that they resort to eating disorders. One is the whole area of competition and success. It is usual to think about men's difficulties with success in terms of the relationship with their fathers: 'Am I as good as Dad? Can I be as successful and not feel I am attacking him? Can I be successful without guilt? Do I have to make sure that I am less successful for fear of his envy?', and so on. But these issues are very much around for women and their mothers too, although it is often more difficult to detect, because competition between women is so little acknowledged. On the whole women seem to find such difficulty with the idea of competition that they even deny it exists. They can do this in numerous ways, the most obvious of which is simply to refuse to compete. The refusal to compete stems from a fear of success or failure; it is not that they are not competitive but they are afraid of competition. Now, this is not to say that women do not have great talent for collaboration. The women's movement particularly has shown that women can co-operate successfully to achieve a common goal. However, women perhaps don't help themselves by failing to know much about their competitiveness.

One of the moments when this question of competition can arise is at puberty. As daughters we are no longer children but developing young women. It is a commonplace that this often happens just as our mothers are nearing the end of their procreative lives. It can be very painful for a woman who is conscious of the ageing process really taking hold – on her skin, her muscle tone, her energy levels – to be faced with a nubile young body and a flirtatious young woman where it seems that only yesterday there was a grubby little girl. Daughters are often acutely aware of their mother's feelings and may decide that it is just not safe or possible to offer a challenge. The obvious way to sidestep the issue is for the daughter to cease to offer competition by getting either fat or very thin and thus defer the whole issue of competition.

This way of competing with our bodies and our appearance is also felt to be very dangerous because women's sense of themselves, their feelings, their identity are all almost inseparable from their bodily awareness. For many women their capacity to like themselves depends very heavily on how they look. This does not seem to be the same for men. They seem much more able to value themselves as distinct from the way they look. So there occurs that phenomenon which so enrages women that a fat man who stinks of body odour will make a pass at a woman. How dare he feel that he is all right and acceptable when he is so ugly and smells bad? In recent years western culture has become steadily more 'lookist'. More and more value is placed on appearance, especially body size and shape. Increasingly, this also applies to young men. In popular culture huge emphasis is placed on how a young person looks rather than on who they are or what they can do.

The competition between fathers and sons often seems to be carried out in action, in who can win. So boys compete with their fathers to win at tennis, at chess, at making money, and in finding sexual partners (just like mother). These limited areas of competition probably have the advantage of not seeming to lay everything on the line: 'Well, he may be able to beat me at tennis, but I know a lot more than him about the stock market.' The danger of the competition between mothers and daughters, perhaps, is that it seems to be about who we are, about everything. If as daughters we sense that our mothers can't stand the competition, or if we ourselves feel unready to take it on, we may have to take evasive action. One way of doing that is to gain or lose weight. Weight gain at this age and stage is so common that we even have a name for it — 'puppy fat'. Of course there is an ordinary and appropriate weight gain at this stage of our development brought about by hormonal changes, but our difficulties in becoming very obviously our mother's rival may well have something to do with considerable weight gain or loss.

However, there can also be difficulties of competition between daughters and mothers over accomplishment and achievement, just as there are between sons and fathers. One client of mine had a mother who was an extremely successful musician. Her daughter, Hilary, was herself talented in several artistic fields, as a singer, a dancer, an actress (but not, interestingly, as a musician). From childhood it had been expected that she would do something very remarkable as a performing artist. Her chief interest when I knew her was in dance, but she was prevented from becoming anything like as good as she might have been by her eating disorder which was so severe and had gone on for so long that it seriously threatened her health. By vomiting and laxative abuse she had so much depleted her body of vital minerals that her health was severely undermined. This stopped her dancing. The issue seemed to be whether, with such a distinguished mother and such expectations of her, Hilary could dare to compete.

Much more often our mothers have accomplished very little in any professional or career sense. This can nonetheless place a heavy burden on us, for anything we accomplish in that way will surpass their achievement. Perhaps we fear their envy, fear our own wish to do better, and that may be partly why so many women finish a training or an education and then do nothing with it. Many women seem to use eating disorders to get themselves out of training or education. It seems an awful lot safer to fail, and interestingly mothers are the ones who say, 'Never mind. I just want you to be happy.' Fathers tend to say, 'I think you should finish the year.'

If we put these dynamics in attachment terms we can say that where mother and daughter are securely attached they both have a sense of their own unique identity and of their difference from each other. Although the bond between them is strong and they are both capable of interest and concern about one another, they can also separate and enjoy their independence. Where the attachment bond is insecure, both mothers and daughters can feel that their identity depends on the other person and then difference, independence and separation become alarming because they threaten security and sense of self. When they both feel secure, achievement becomes a matter for congratulation rather than a threat to the other.

The Legacy of Anger

Many women carry rage with them about their mothers. Some of that is probably built in. Mothers are extremely powerful in the lives of young children and it would be an extraordinary child who did not have a legacy of anger and dissatisfaction. Indeed, it is probably necessary for mothers to fail their children to some degree, to be unsatisfactory, or otherwise girls would never leave home. But many women seem to have the memory of real and significant bad treatment and don't know what to do with the feelings they retain from those times. They have great difficulty with their rage with their mothers and often direct it against themselves. You may remember the story of Isobel who got back at her mean mother by gorging packets of biscuits.

Another woman, Susan, had been trained up from an early age to be a dancer. When she was a child and teenager her mother, who was significantly overweight, had deprived Susan of food to keep her thin for dancing: 'No, Susan, no ice cream for you. Have an apple.' Mother had wanted to be a dancer herself and it looked as though Susan had the job of being both thin and a dancer for her mother. Not surprisingly this created enormous rage and resentment in Susan, but while she was at home she was too frightened to be able to express it, although there were lots of rows about food and Susan's secret sweet eating. When she left home she began to put on weight to such an extent that her ability to go on dancing was at risk. There was tremendous secret satisfaction for Susan in seeing how she could enrage and pay back her mother for what she had put her through simply by eating the things she had been deprived of for all those long years. However, it was some time before she could see that, and even longer before she could separate out whether it was only her mother who wanted her to dance. Her fury with her mother was bringing her to destroy her dancing before she had really considered whether she might like it for herself.

One woman, Theresa, whose beginnings had not been happy, had a mother who was so bossy and interfering that she would even demand that her daughter talk when mother thought she should. Of course that created a real game between them when Theresa discovered she could wind her mother up just by not saying anything. There was a lot of real unhappiness for Theresa which she dealt with by getting very thin. In due course she left home and when she went back to visit used to raid the refrigerator and eat voraciously. It seemed as though she was trying to express all her hatred and anger with the mother who didn't love her well enough by stealing other kinds of nourishment.

Over and over again we can see that when mothers have been unable to respond well enough to their daughters, the language that gets used to express the daughters' unhappiness and dissatisfaction is the language of food.

Stop and Think

Could it be that your use of food is the way you have chosen to manage the feelings to do with your mother? If your stomach could speak to your mother, what would it say?

The Need to Separate

Some perspective on all these examples of mother/daughter relationships can be gained if they are placed in the context of the major issue for mothers and growing daughters: that of separation. The question for all mothers is: 'Can I let my daughter go with my blessing to live her life as well as she can and for herself?' The question for all daughters is: 'Can I let my mother go and live as well as I can and for myself?'

Often when people hear the word 'separation' they seem to imagine some final parting, some absolute ending. Indeed, men have often been praised for what is seen as their ability to leave their mothers behind and go off and live their lives. More recently, however, people have begun to wonder whether men's much vaunted independence comes from an organic process of emotional growth, or from a cutting off and denial of feelings. It is becoming ever clearer that men often rely on women to do all kinds of emotional work for them, and by that means avoid much of the pain of feelings. On the other hand, women have often been criticised for failing to separate and for holding on to what seems an inappropriately 'childish' role, especially in relation to their mothers. For instance, I heard a conversation on the bus one day where a couple in their sixties were talking about their grown-up daughter, married and with children. What they described was a total dependency: 'She phones up and she's round to us for the least little thing. If anything happens,' said her mother, 'she wants me to be round to her.' It seemed as though, in this case, no psychological separation whatever had taken place. Recent thinking has suggested that independence and individuation for women are not and probably will never be the kind of ruthless detachment that men so often seem to practise. In their growing up, women have developed an ability for connectedness which is a strength and of great importance.

So then, what does it mean to talk about women separating from their mothers? It means mothers and daughters reaching an understanding that they are two separate individuals. At one level, of course, this is blindingly obvious, but at another it is not. They are not separate if the inner and emotional lives of mother and daughter are still tangled up together. In all the situations that were described earlier, this was the case. All of those daughters were behaving in ways that were to do with their mothers rather than with themselves. They were unable to be clear about what they wanted and what was for their own good as distinct from their mothers'. In a way they were living in this respect as if they and their mothers were the same person, a single unit, unseparated.

The issue of separation for women is a complex one – too complex to explore in detail here except for two points. One is that it demands from us a process of mourning and letting go. The mourning is for what has been good and belongs to a stage of our life now over and also for what has not been right and for what we have not been given. A lot of our holding on is in the hope that we will finally get what we feel we never had enough of: love, approval, whatever it might be. A lot of women I have worked with have returned over and over again to bad situations and come away battered. The revisiting is in the unconscious hope that this time it will be different: 'This time I will get what I want; this time my mother will be the way I want her to be.' But we also need to mourn the ending of a part of our lives and a stage of our development in order to be able to take on the challenges of adult life. The letting go has to be a mutual process. Separation is a two-way street, with some sadness in it for both mother and daughter.

Chapter Eight
Eating Your Heart Out

"I eat only to fill the hole in my heart."
— Compulsive eater

So far several possible meanings have been explored that singly or in combination may be at the root of an eating disorder. They have been considered as a response to crisis, as a reaction to the social role demanded of women, as a holding pattern in dealing with sexuality and growing up, as a means of self-assertion in a life that feels overcontrolled by others, and as a means of coping with the relationship with our mothers. However, there are other ways of understanding these problems. One of these is based on the premise that both the ravenous craving that results in compulsive eating and the violent denial of hunger that results in anorexia can be physical expressions of terrible emotional emptiness that there seems no way of soothing or satisfying.

The roots of this hunger, this emptiness, are most often to be found in early experience that has not been good enough to enable a person to grow up with a full feeling of being loved and valued.[1] Jennifer was a young woman whose childhood had been spent between her mother and her grandmother. At the age of three family circumstances had meant that her mother could no longer look after her and she had been sent to live with her grandmother. This in itself was bad enough since other children in the family stayed with her mother, but her grandmother was also a harsh and unloving woman with whom Jennifer was very unhappy. Jennifer was also a person of considerable strength and determination; she survived this beginning and used her anger about it to make a success. On the outside she appeared a cheerful, well-organised and ambitious young woman. On the inside, however, there was a part of her that was a desperately unhappy and unloved child. When that part of her was touched by some incident during the day she would be overcome by the most appalling cravings and feelings of emptiness. Jennifer felt these to be a craving for food and would binge voraciously and desperately, but at the same time she would know with part of her that it was not food she was hungry for but something else.

That something else is often identified as sex. Penny was a young woman whose parents had separated when she was quite small. The children had stayed with their mother who had remarried. By this second husband she had had other children. Penny was violently jealous of these half-siblings because she felt rejected by her mother. As a teenager she went off in a rage to live with her father, but he too had remarried and Penny could not make a relationship with his second wife and other children. The poor girl felt she had no parents and no home. At that time when she was quite young, only about 16, she found a boyfriend. Alan was a capable, successful and gentle man a few years older, who was prepared to take care of Penny. What neither one of them was prepared for was the weight of dependency that Penny very soon began to place on him. Alan became the absolute centre of her universe. She resented his absence at work, but even more his absences when he went to play squash and meet his friends. She had an insatiable need to be cuddled and comforted and attended to by him. This need was often felt to be sexual so that a great deal of lovemaking went on between them. Nevertheless, sex left her feeling empty and unsatisfied, wanting more – although she could not identify what that 'more' was.

Alan told Penny that he felt that if she could, she would get right inside him. During his absence this emptiness, this craving, could become unbearable and would be experienced by Penny as a compulsive need to eat. She would then binge and vomit. At other times she would protect herself from these feelings by total self-sufficiency and in these moods would triumphantly do all sorts of things that she was usually afraid to do on her own. At these times she would also stop eating.

What Penny was in touch with was the painful truth that her relationship with her boyfriend could not satisfy needs that dated from much earlier in her life. With part of her she was a baby needing a mother; a sexual relationship touched on those same needs for intimacy, dependency, loving and holding, but because she was not in fact a baby with her mother, but a young woman in a relationship with another young adult, those needs could never be properly satisfied. An adult sexual relationship is not, so to speak, designed to do that job, although it can certainly from time to time satisfy some of the residual infant needs of an adult. For the same reason, and much more obviously, infant needs cannot be met by bingeing. On the other hand, those infant needs cannot be denied by starvation – or at least not without paying a price so high that it makes nonsense of starvation as a way of coping.

It is important for those of us for whom life falls apart in our late teens or early twenties, to be able to recognise that we did the best job we could in surviving what was not good in our childhoods. If we need to do some repair work it is hardly surprising and not something that should be a source of shame. We did not create the difficulties of our early lives. It was not Jennifer's fault that her mother could not look after her, or that her grandmother was cruel and unloving. It was not Penny's fault that her parents divorced and remarried and that Penny was faced with tremendous difficulties in knowing where she belonged. The task that lies before us when our ways of coping stop working is to try and repair some of that early damage. Exactly the same attitude should be taken if you have been overcome by your eating behaviour at a later stage of your development. You managed the pressures upon you the best way you could. If you now want to find other ways of coping, be proud that you have that impulse to health.

A Signal for Change

The sign that time for repair work has come for some people is an eating disorder. Why? Why should that symptom have anything to do with what has gone on for us as children and growing up? The answer may lie in the associations of food and eating that were discussed in Chapter 2. The links between feeling physically full/empty and emotionally full/empty are extremely close, so close that many of us cannot tell the difference between them. We cannot tell the difference between emotional anguish and hunger; we cannot tell the difference between denying our physical hunger and denying our emotional emptiness. We eat to fill the hole in our hearts. We translate into eating behaviour all the painfulness of our emotional state. So we can try and satisfy our emotional emptiness by eating food we don't want, then angrily deny our need for love by forcing food out of our bodies, then furiously refuse to acknowledge that we need love or people at all by starving ourselves and cutting ourselves off from the feelings of hunger and of need.

Often the problem for those with backgrounds of early deprivation is not simply that they want to be loved and cherished. The problem is that they want to be loved and cherished, but that simultaneously they are terrified that those who say they love them in fact do not, and will betray them. The meaning they make of their early experience is that their trust and love was betrayed. They think it is much too dangerous to love. They want to, some of the time, but they get terribly frightened, so frightened that they retreat, back off, withdraw, or attack and destroy. In fact they are so frightened that they do not consciously know much about this process in emotional terms at all. Instead they experience it, they live it, in terms of food and eating. They live their emotional lives in terms of food.

So what am I suggesting? I am suggesting that eating disorders are not only hell in themselves but that there is no hope in them. They do nothing for us; in fact they do worse than nothing, they actually compound our misery. We may therefore come to that point where we are willing to try an alternative which might have some hope attached to it. In my view that alternative is to begin to think and feel about our beginnings, our early experience, our past lives in the context of a safe relationship with another person, probably a professional. This will not be easy, nor will it be painless. In fact it may well prove an exceedingly painful process. However, as has been suggested already, the pain of our underlying difficulties may not be worse than the pain of our eating disorder solution. In many situations I believe that to be true. I see lots of women for whom facing the underlying issues is a great relief. They are literally fed up to the back teeth with food misuse. The kind of feeling and crying that facing their problems arouses in them and is shared with me may be painful, but it is nothing in comparison to the torment of food misuse.

For those with very long-standing difficulties of early deprivation there is no guarantee that the pain of knowing about all that will be less. It may be just as bad as they fear. However, it does have two very valuable hopes attached to it. One hope is that facing the past will bring an end to the eating disorder, and the other is that it is a process that will accomplish something much more fundamental: it will enable them to lay the ghosts of the past to rest. Eating disorders have no hope and no end. If you recognise yourself in all this, it is very likely that you are going to need some help. The resources in Chapter 12 include a description of the kind of help there is available, but let me tell you first how it went for one young woman with this kind of very difficult problem to resolve.

Angela's Story

The first public sign of Angela's falling apart was her failure to come to college. It was not the hiccup in attendance that is experienced by anyone who has an ordinary bad day, but the paralysing inability for weeks on end to get into college for more than one or two days a week. She was fortunate in a way that she was a student at a dance school. In such institutions there is a great stress on attendance because improvement depends on consistent, regular, daily work. Her absence was noted as it might not have been had she been following some other course of study. She was urged to find some help and because there was a bit of her that was frightened and wanted to get better she did.

As she started to talk it became clear that Angela's public statement of her difficulties by her absence had come at the end of a long period of great pain and misery. Angela was bulimic. When the craving to eat came upon her she would stuff herself with whatever she could find until her abdomen was distended and painful. Then she would make herself sick. Exhausted by all this she would fall asleep. In a really bad episode she could spend days and nights like this, losing all sense of time. Once she began to binge and feel disgusted with herself, she was overtaken by a frenzy of hatred for herself that locked her ever tighter into her eating and vomiting.

When it was all over, she would feel physically exhausted and emotionally devastated. She would sleep and wake up feeling it had been the most horrific bad dream. But the battered state of her digestive system, the bags under her eyes, the foul taste in her mouth were evidence that this was no dream. She was ashamed to be with people when she looked so bad. Her abdomen was swollen; fluid retention made her whole body puffy. There was no way she could put on a leotard and do her dance classes. So she stayed away from school. Sometimes she would then move into an anorexic phase and within a day or so would begin to feel strong and in control so that she could return to school. Sometimes she would spend the day in bed reading compulsively so that she need not think about anything; sometimes, as she read, she would eat biscuits, not acknowledging to herself what she was doing until she again felt sick and bloated.

Not surprisingly there was very little room for ordinary life in this way of living. There was certainly no room for a sexual relationship; there was barely room for friendships. Angela had a terrible guilty secret about food and what she did with it. She felt very, very ashamed and she judged and condemned herself, and she imagined that anyone who knew would do the same. She could only be with her friends when her eating felt under control, which was less and less often. In any case social occasions very often involved eating and drinking, so they were themselves difficult. When Angela wasn't actually bingeing, her hope and intention was not to eat anything, so going out for a meal with friends held nothing but terror for her. Not surprisingly, her friends felt upset and rejected by her behaviour and gradually had less and less to do with her. Bit by bit she became more and more isolated and more and more preoccupied with food. It was at this point that she began the pattern of absenteeism which finally brought her to somebody's attention.

Whatever was all this torment about? Well, for some considerable time Angela felt that it was about itself. In other words the problem for Angela lay in the eating disorder and the consequences that followed from it. However incomplete this view may be, it does need to be treated with respect for two reasons. One is that there is the possibility of physical illness causing these symptoms, and that possibility, however small, needs to be eliminated. Angela's visit to the doctor revealed a body suffering from the brutal punishment that it had been given, but otherwise healthy. Second, any person with an eating disorder has before her the preliminary task of consciously acknowledging that there is a problem. It is not for nothing that Alcoholics Anonymous insists on members publicly acknowledging the difficulty whenever they speak in a meeting: 'My name is X; I am an alcoholic.' Until a person with an eating disorder is able to recognise consciously what she is doing to herself, she is unlikely to be able to stop.

When a person with an eating disorder seeks help in counselling or therapy, she needs the opportunity to discover that she will not be treated with the contempt and judgement that she doles out to herself on a daily basis. Unless there can be that much safety and acceptance, she is most unlikely to say any more about anything. Gradually, Angela began to be able to trust the counselling space and to allow us both to know about a lot of awful things that had happened to her and that still bothered her a great deal.

This was a painful process. Sometimes Angela lost sight of me as someone who was on her side. I became the judging, condemning, rejecting person that she was so often to herself. For a long time, whenever she had a binge she would stay away because she imagined that I was going to hate, attack and despise her for it, the way she hated, attacked and despised herself. With part of her she needed and loved and trusted me, but with another part she was terrified of that dependence and really frightened that I was not her friend as she sometimes thought and believed, but her judge and her tormentor. It took a long time for that to change.

What family background had produced this much fear and how could Angela's eating disorder be understood? What was it for? How was it supposed to help? Angela was the eldest of four children. Her parents had married when they were still only teenagers and Angela had been born within the year. Two other girls had soon followed and then after a gap of three years there was a boy. Her mother had had a less than wonderful start in life which made the considerable difficulties of dealing with a baby while she herself was still not 20 even worse. The arrival very soon afterwards of other children would have been a challenge to the most secure and stable woman.

It was not possible to know very much about what happened in Angela's babyhood and up to the age of about five, but from what she did remember and had been told, by the time she went to school she was a precociously independent little girl. She behaved like someone of 5 going on 15. From the beginning she took herself to school, went to the local shops, looked after her younger siblings. How was this premature abandonment of babyhood and childhood to be understood?

Angela did not believe that she was allowed to be a baby or a little girl with needs appropriate to her age. Presumably she had come to this conclusion because in fact her overstretched mother found it difficult to respond to those needs. Angela's mother needed this eldest child of hers to grow up almost as soon as she was born and Angela had done what she could to oblige.

But there was a further complication. The second child, also a girl, Mary, was from the beginning 'difficult' which meant that she protested and complained a great deal. Whatever attention was available from Angela's mother was hogged by Mary. Even as the babies grew a bit older Angela did not benefit. If anyone's baby needs were going to be attended to, Mary made sure it would be hers. This of course was good for Mary and appropriate behaviour for a child who was being deprived, but it was not good news for Angela.

There was not even much to be hoped for from Angela's father. The frustrations and difficulties of his life combined to make him explosively bad-tempered. His violent rages were often directed at Angela who was terrified by him. At the same time, in other moods he would talk to Angela, then about 12, about the difficulties in his relationship with her mother. Eventually she was also the one who was told about his affair. She was, of course, sworn to secrecy. This combination of seductive excitement in the relationship with her father, alternating with fear of his rages, was not at all easy to deal with.

How was Angela going to cope with all this? She was an intelligent child with a powerful personality, so she survived what might have destroyed anyone not so strong. She became the determined, capable, cheerful one in the family. That, of course, made life easy for Angela's family but left her extremely isolated. There was no one, and never really had been anyone, who could respond fully to her emotional needs. She learned very early to take care of herself and her own needs. As she got into her teens her friendships with both boys and girls were usually based on Angela's capacity to look after them. In the only important relation- ship with a boy, things worked out well while Angela remained cheerful and capable. When the desperately deprived child part of her peeped out, her boyfriend responded with fear and outrage.

It was probably the breaking up of this relationship combined with the move away from home to college that sparked off Angela's eating disorder. Another young woman might have had a breakdown or become very depressed. Angela began a pattern of food misuse that fitted in with the needs of her family for her not to be overtly demanding. Food was the 'feeder without feeling', the inanimate mother to meet her needs. By this time she had in any case learned her lesson well and had discovered how not to let herself know about her emotional needs. So at that point it did not seem to her as though a lot of problems from the past had finally caught up with her. Rather, it seemed that she was mysteriously unable to control her weight. She was starting on the path that finally brought her to seek some assistance three years later.

How could all of this be helped? Well, for one thing there was a lot of crying to be done and a lot of anger to be expressed. Throughout her life Angela had either repressed these feelings or more recently expressed them in food misuse. As she grew more able to believe that I could stand her feelings, she began to believe she could bear them too. Feelings could be expressed and shared with less fear of damaging or disastrous consequences to either of us. Inevitably that meant she had less need to misuse food; she did not need her inanimate feeder anymore and the strength began to ebb away from that compulsion.

Second, there was a lot of thinking and feeling and understanding for us to do together about how Angela's early life had influenced her. It was not only that on any objective scale her growing up had taken place in difficult circumstances – that certainly needed to be remembered and pondered. What was also important was to understand what Angela had made of all that. For example, Angela believed (without consciously knowing it) that her mother had not been able to bear her feelings (which was probably true) and that therefore no one else could either. Consequently she had to take care of them herself. Was that true? Was it true as far as I was concerned? And if it was not true for me, might it be that it was not true for other people either? This enquiry had direct bearing on Angela's eating disorder because it opened the way towards the possibility of trusting and mutual relationships in which the feelings and needs of both parties could be acknowledged. The need for the lonely and isolated eating behaviour solution became less acute.

But there was a further and very important process at work as Angela and I continued to talk. I became very important for Angela because I was able to do and be for her a person of a kind she had never experienced enough of before. I listened to her, I focused on her, I thought about her and remembered her when we were not together, I attended to her and in so doing recognised and validated her as a precious human being. I did not do any of this perfectly, or without mistakes or lapses, but I did it better than it had been done for her before. In an important way I became a mother for Angela, since that is what ordinary good mothers do – they attend to their children's emotional (and physical) needs.

As our relationship continued and deepened Angela became more able to believe that I would be available to her emotionally when she came to see me. This had important practical effects in making her eating disorder less necessary, but it also created something different in the way Angela could be to herself. One way of saying it would be like this: Angela's mother had in some important ways not been good enough for Angela, so Angela had never had modelled ways of being good to herself. She was as careless and neglectful of her own feelings as her mother had been – indeed probably considerably more careless and neglectful. But I was not careless and neglectful of her feelings. On the contrary, to the best of my ability I gave them close and careful attention. Gradually Angela learned to do the same and came to believe that what went on inside her was worthy of attention and respect. She began to be able to pay attention to the screams and yells of the infant/child part of herself.

What this meant was that although there was quite a long period of time in which Angela dared to feel quite dependent on me – and therefore vulnerable to the pain of absence between sessions and during holidays – yet she was engaged in a process of growth which gradually enabled her to develop her own good mother inside her and so have less need of me. By that time attacks on herself by bingeing, vomiting and starving were no longer part of the way she treated herself.

At that point Angela came to the end of her course and therefore to the end of our time together, since I was the student counsellor. We had worked for almost three years, mostly once a week, during the most difficult time twice a week, and in occasional times of crisis more often. We had accomplished a great deal together. Neither of us would say it had been easy, painless or at times even pleasant. There had been no inevitable trajectory of progress. Rather there had been quite a few bumps, lurches and hiccups. Furthermore, neither of us believed that Angela was now beginning a pain-free existence. On the contrary, she was beginning a life in which she would be free to feel her pain instead of translating it into eating behaviour. Nor had we together dealt with all the issues that were difficult for Angela. If circumstances had permitted we might have gone on longer, but in a way we had done enough. Angela was ready to leave home in a way that she had not been ready to leave her parental home. She wanted to try her wings and she had some confidence that this time they would be strong enough to let her soar.

So where does that leave you, the reader? I hope it does not leave you thinking that a miracle was accomplished for Angela. It was no miracle; it was the result of a lot of hard work over a long period for both of us. It gives you an idea of just how much effort goes into trying to deal with and mend things that have not been good enough in our early lives. Sadly, there is no magic and no instant cure.

Second, things don't always go easily. Angela and I had a fairly bumpy ride together. Sometimes it doesn't work out and the therapeutic relationship comes to a premature end. Rosie was someone who found the whole process of looking at what her bingeing and laxative abuse might be about unbearably painful. She wanted to think about it, but it was at that time just too awful. She tried over quite a long period of time, but it was too hard. She left the college and I lost track of her. Two years later I met her quite by chance and she told me that she had found a therapist with whom she had been working for the past six months and that things were beginning to come together for her. I was extremely pleased because it made me feel that although what Rosie and I had done together had not in any ordinary sense been a 'success', it had been good enough for her to feel that it was worth another try. To dare to confront the wounds of our early lives takes a lot of courage from both parties. It is a difficult and painful process, but it has some hope attached to it and food misuse has none.

Do the stories in this chapter enable you to recognise that your eating behaviour is a reaction to the difficulties you experienced while you were growing up? If so, you have a number of choices. I briefly describe below the range of the kinds of help that can be given. More details are given in the resources in Chapter 12. The main point I want to make to you, however, is that you have had very good reason to use food to help you manage. If you want to find another less damaging way of dealing with the hand that life has dealt you, you will need to learn how to take care of yourself and use other people rather than food to make life bearable.

- You can try and work on your own history by yourself. There are plenty of self-help books you could work through. Some of these are described in Chapter 12, but you can probably find others. Be aware that this can be a lonely journey and at some point you may want to seek the help of others.
- Second, you can find self-help groups that have the advantage of giving you a space to hear how other people have managed and provide support for you. B-eat (formerly the Eating Disorders Association) organises groups of this kind all over the country. I provide groups for people who regard themselves as emotional eaters via Understanding Your Eating. You can also find groups that will help you deal with

the consequences of having a parent or sibling with problems of addiction, such as Al-Anon or Al-Ateen which help the families of alcoholics. These groups can have the disadvantage that you have limited space for the exploration of your own difficulties, although you may very well benefit from hearing about other people's.

- Third, you can look for one-to-one help. This need not be formal paid counselling; some schools have excellent pastoral care systems. Some churches can offer this kind of support. Some youth workers and social workers will provide help of this kind. There is also formal counselling. More details are given in Chapter 12.

Chapter Nine
....
Eating Disorders as a Response to Sexual Abuse

"Anorexia, like compulsive eating, is an attempt to protect yourself, to assert control. . . . You are trying to regain the power that was taken from you as a child."

— Ellen Bass and Laura Davis,
The Courage to Heal, 1988

Over the past 20 years it has become very much more obvious that many children are sexually abused, and what the devastating emotional effects of such abuse can be. It has also become clearer that many women use preoccupation with food, size and shape as a way of coping with a history of sexual abuse.[1] In this chapter I want to discuss first of all how women that I have worked with have used eating disorders to deal with the memory and the fact of sexual abuse, and second how they have used eating disorders to cope with the effects of sexual abuse on their day-to-day functioning.

Remembering but not Feeling

I have worked with a number of women who were abused as children and have never forgotten that fact, but who have used eating disorders as a way of keeping the feelings about the abuse away from them. These women can talk about the abuse, but it is as if it happened to someone else.

Carla's Story

Carla had been regularly and systematically raped by her uncle over a period of years. There had been no one that she could tell, so she was left to deal with this awful reality on her own. Her mother was a frightening woman, capable of awful rages and very unpredictable. Her father was absent, making money. Carla was the eldest child and unable to confide in her younger siblings. She was in a terrible situation and it is not surprising that she needed some extreme way of dealing with it. For some years she transferred her anxiety, fear and disgust into the fantasy that she was HIV positive. Eventually, in her early twenties, she had the courage to get herself tested and found that she was not and never had been HIV positive. But this discovery left her without a means of protecting herself from feelings that she could not yet tolerate. She 'chose' instead (but not of course in any conscious way) anorexia as another way of displacing her fears. Carla was one of those anorexics who was not so much preoccupied with counting calories as maintaining an anorexic way of life. She starved herself of food (no breakfast, no time for lunch or just a quick sandwich, dinner if her husband made it, or just a drink and a few peanuts) and she was very thin. But she also starved herself of sleep, of warmth (she didn't wear enough clothes), of pleasure (life was just work), of a social life and in fact of everything that makes life pleasurable and enjoyable. If occasionally she did allow herself some minor treat, such as lying in for an hour, she felt that she had been 'selfish', and then she had to make up for that lapse by more than ordinary efforts. This system took up every shred of Carla's energy and attention so that she couldn't possibly come into contact with the feelings relating to the abuse she had suffered. The road to acknowledging those feelings and working through them was a long one, and it began with Carla gradually being able to recognise simple feelings in her body such as tiredness and hunger. The feelings relating to the incest were so terrible that she had had to find a way of deadening herself to all feeling.

Remembering and not Remembering

Other women with whom I have worked have had the suspicion, the feeling, the faint memory of something awful that happened. They aren't sure what it was exactly; they worry that maybe they made it up or imagined it; it comes back to them in dreams and momentary flashbacks. But they have nothing firm or concrete to go on. Some people – therapists, judges, social workers, parents – find it easy to accuse women of 'making things up'. Children have been known to describe quite explicitly how they have been abused, only to be told that they are bad for making things up. That children or women might do this has always seemed very unlikely to me. I don't find the women I work with full of fantastic invention, rather the reverse. They are concerned with finding the truth and afraid of exaggerating or fantasising what has happened to them. I think you can take any suspicions you have that you may have been abused very seriously indeed. However, these suspicions are extremely painful and disturbing, and women will often work hard to distract themselves from persistent worries. Eating disorders are one of the ways women use to do this.

Philippa's Story

Philippa was someone who slept very badly and had recurring dreams that woke her up in a state of panic. One of these dreams was that a man was pushing something down her throat, trying to suffocate her. She also had a whole range of 'daydreams' that came to her when she was between sleeping and waking: one was that a man was coming upstairs and into her room; another was that she was lying in bed and a man was in the same bed with her and she could feel his erect penis against her buttocks. This last was not the ordinary pleasant sexual fantasy of the grown woman, but the terrifying anxiety of the child. Were these dreams some indication of a reality that Philippa did not remember? For many years she had been too terrified of these shadows to allow herself to consider them. Instead she had filled every waking moment with worries about food, shape and size. Philippa was a compulsive eater and stuffed down her suspicions and her memories with the food she ate. Only in her dreams and half-waking state did these persistent images come back to haunt her. I was the first person to whom she had confided these suspicions and I took them very seriously. They made sense to me in terms of what I already knew about Philippa's family. We began to work on these images by saying: 'If this is an accurate memory, what do you think it means? If this is an accurate memory what was happening? If this is an accurate memory what does it explain in the present and about how you are now? If this is an accurate memory, what feelings go with it?'

By these means we began to understand more about Philippa's experience and inner world. Then she began to say, without any prompting from me, that she thought she really didn't need to binge in the way she had, so that gradually over time she gave up having to cope by bingeing. She continued to work on her feelings, thoughts and memories, but she no longer needed to translate her distress into food misuse.

Forgetting

Quite often people come into counselling complaining of something, for instance, an eating disorder, and feel that the complaint is the 'real' problem. This is the 'If only I were ten pounds lighter then my life would be perfect' syndrome, and usually covers all sorts of other worries and fears. As counselling proceeds these underlying issues become clearer, and people frequently remember all sorts of things they had 'forgotten'. So far as neuroscience can tell us it seems highly unlikely that we truly 'forget' anything. Even those experiences that date from before words and the full development of our brains seem to leave traces and feelings behind. It has, for example, proved well worthwhile for some people to attempt to reconstruct their birth experience, of which they have no 'memory' in the most obvious sense.

When we feel safe and understood and not judged, we can have access to all sorts of memories and feelings that otherwise we keep well hidden, even from ourselves. It is in this way that memories of sexual abuse sometimes surface when they have previously not been available to conscious memory. Beverley was one such person.

Beverley's Story

Beverley had grown up in a household where there was a lot of violence and had suffered a particularly unpleasant childhood. She was a compulsive eater and had been for as long as she could remember, and apparently for a very good reason. In her twenties she joined a group for compulsive eaters and began to work on the underlying problems and difficulties in her life. She found the group helpful and through it came to the realisation that she was not alone in her compulsive eating and that she could learn from other people's memories and experience. Bit by bit she remembered many things she had forgotten from her childhood which up to that point had been very shadowy, with lots of gaps. Among other things, she gradually remembered that her father had sexually abused her from when she was still quite small, over a period of several years. There was no doubt in her mind about these memories; she remembered all kinds of details that fixed them in time and place, but up until then they had been totally absent from her conscious mind. Of course, it was not easy to have these things coming back to mind and Beverley got very upset about it on many occasions and for a long time afterwards. However, it was also a relief because it explained aspects of her behaviour that she had never really been able to understand before, including her fear of sexual relationships with men.

This theme of relief is not uncommon when women remember things that have been long forgotten. Hannah, like Beverley, had been physically abused as a child by both her parents. She had never forgotten those experiences, or the fear and rage that went with the memories. However, she had a long history of a troubled relationship with food and size and had first been anorexic for several years, and then bulimic. When I got to know her we spent a lot of time working through her relationship with her parents. This helped the bulimia but did not really get rid of it. However, when she began to remember the way her grandfather had sexually abused her she uncovered a whole area of feeling and experience that had previously been hidden. Then she began to understand more about the way she related to men in the present and more about her relationship with her parents and their relationship with their parents. This was extremely painful for Hannah, but also hailed a very creative period, which brought an end to the bulimia once and for all.

Sexual Relationships and Intimacy with Men

It is not unknown for women to abuse children sexually and it is certainly not unknown for boys to be abused, but in this chapter I am focusing on the sexual abuse of girls by men, and in this section on the effects that the abuse has in the day-to-day lives of those abused girls once they grow up. Perhaps the most obvious and easy to understand of the effects of sexual abuse are the problems it causes many women in forming adult sexual relationships. These problems are often disguised for a long time by eating disorders.

One woman, a compulsive eater for many years, described herself as someone who had had 'lots of sex but not much love'. As a child she had been given sex rather than love, but of course her need as a child was for love, and not for sex. The two were hopelessly confused in her mind. Somewhere inside her she thought that if she had sex she would get love. She had been an unloved child, like most victims of incest, and had complied with the demands of her abuser in the desperate need for and hope of some sort of attention. In her adult life she did the same. Out of desperate need she engaged in any sexual liaison that was on offer and again found herself unloved. Instead, she found comfort the only way she knew, with food. She thought the only thing about her that anyone wanted was her sexual availability, since that was what she had been wanted for as a child, so she hid from herself with food the painful feelings of worthlessness that easily overcame her. This story has a sad ending however. This woman was in her forties; she had been living like this for 25 years. For her to develop would have involved an enormous change in her whole existence and way of life; it would have been a long and painful business. Evidently it seemed too difficult, at least just then in that way, because I only ever saw her once. Maybe she went away and worked on it all on her own, maybe she found someone else to help her. I hope so.

It's not uncommon for young people who come from unloving backgrounds to engage in sexual relations while they are still very young. We live in a culture that sexualises clothing and behaviour from an early age and we allow our young people freedoms that permit early sexual relations. But these relationships are often built on the mistaken belief that unmet child need can be repaired with sex. It is true that adult sexual relationships can repair childhood deficits, but only when the sexual relationship is in the context of love, concern and mutual respect. Girls (and perhaps some boys) who engage in sex very early may well find themselves feeling not loved and restored but used and abused.

The opposite extreme from trying to find love through sex is to abolish all thoughts of sex or interest in it. This is the solution to the trauma of sexual abuse that I have known a number of women find through anorexia. Anorexia produces a state of starvation, which has the physiological effect of forcing our bodies to focus on survival rather than reproduction. It alters a woman's hormone balance and makes her infertile – as if her body knows it cannot sustain a foetus. This combines with a lack of sexual feelings or fantasies. Not only that, anorexia is, and is meant to be, a very preoccupying state of mind. You have to work very hard to be an anorexic. You certainly haven't got the time or the energy to be thinking about sex. The only trouble with this solution is that it is a terrible way to live and an incredibly high price to pay to obliterate the trauma of the original abuse. I have known women spend all the fertile years of their lives in this state, not daring to be sexual because of that original horror and pain with which they first experienced sex.

Exactly the same effect can be achieved by becoming very overweight. Serious obesity reduces fertility, again as if our bodies know that carrying so much weight is not desirable for the wellbeing of the foetus and child. If you are seriously overweight you may also find that sexual relations become practically very difficult. Your fat will literally prevent anyone getting near to you. This may rescue you from intimacy that feels too frightening.

What is commoner, at least in my experience, is for women to have sexual thoughts and feelings, but to have difficulties in actually translating those into a satisfying sexual relationship with a man or woman. These difficulties can be disguised in various ways by eating disorders. Best known of these is: 'I feel fat and ugly. If I didn't feel like that I would be out socialising every night/settling down to a long-term relationship/looking for a sexual partner/enjoying the sexual relationship I have. However, until I have lost weight I can't do this.' While all their attention is focused on their weight these women can avoid facing both the awful truth about the past and the awful truth about the present: that they are afraid of sexual intimacy with another person and that they have good reason to feel like that.

Sometimes these difficulties only emerge when women are actually involved in a relationship and begin to realise, often through reading, that the sexual experience they have within the relationship is not the fulfilling enjoyable experience they hear that other women have. They become aware, for example, that they don't feel anything when they are being caressed intimately, that they switch off from intercourse, that the only way they have orgasms is when they masturbate in private. Sometimes, when they are making love, such women will then have flashbacks to their childhood experience. One woman I worked with had flashbacks to her abusive brother's face, which momentarily displaced her lover. Often these realisations have been held at bay for years by preoccupations with food and size.

Trust and Control

None of these difficulties in sexual function are very easy to deal with or to resolve, especially since what lies behind them are issues of trust and control. In order to have a satisfying sexual relationship we must be able to trust our partner, and to be able to tolerate not being in complete control either of the situation or of ourselves. But by definition, the victim of sexual abuse has had her trust betrayed and has been in a situation where she was not in control but was controlled for another person's use. These issues of trust and control are often central to the emotional development of the abuse survivor.

It is part of the hard work involved in having an intimate relationship to develop trust and mutuality so that neither person in the partnership feels that they are either in control or controlled. However, the person with an eating disorder, especially the sexually abused woman, has moved the issues of trust and control away from a person and a relationship and into the arena of food. For example, a teenager with an eating disorder is not struggling directly with her problems of mistrust and control through her social contacts and friendships. She will almost certainly not be quarrelling with her boyfriend about which film they will go and see or worrying whether a friend has been gossiping behind her back. The tackling of such issues would help her develop skills of negotiation, and a sense of mutuality and trust. However, the eating disordered youngster has little or no social life, falls in with whatever someone else wants to do, instead transferring issues of trust and control on to food. What she mistrusts is the packet of cereal in the cupboard, or the chocolate bar in the shop or the ham sandwich in her stomach. She doesn't know whether these things are good for her or not, and she doesn't know whether she wants to have anything to do with them or not. She thinks about dealing with them by control but she often feels that they control her. She's not anxious about whether she should go out to the cinema with the boy next door, she's anxious about whether she should have the yoghurt that's in the fridge.

One girl who was a student nurse was a very good example of this way of doing things. Instead of having a social life she sat in her room in the hostel, always finding an excuse not to go out with her friends until they grew tired of asking. Part of her wanted to go out to a club on Friday evenings. She had plenty of fantasies about meeting boys, kissing and fondling. But she was also deeply afraid of any kind of real sexual encounter with a man because of the incestuous abuse perpetrated by her father. She couldn't, at this point, bring herself to think about these worries directly, so instead she worried about food. She made herself overweight so then she could spend all her spare time thinking about dieting and/or bingeing, rather than worrying about the fact that she both did and did not want to find a boyfriend who she did and did not want to kiss her.

This same technique of displacement of worries from a person on to food happens in established relationships as well (and by no means only with those who have suffered sexual abuse). When Suzanne disagreed with her partner she didn't argue with her, she went and made herself sick. When she was worried about where she was and what she was doing when she came home late, night after night, she didn't challenge her, she binged instead.

The trouble with this system is not only that the person develops an eating disorder, which is bad enough; not only that they avoid dealing with the original problem, but that they deprive themselves of the emotional experience that everyone needs to make satisfying relationships and to develop within them. It's like having a learning difficulty; you truant from school because you hate reading and the truanting gets you into trouble. Nobody asks why reading has become such a problem for you, but in the meantime you still don't learn to read, which means that all sorts of other activities become impossible as well. Learning to read is not an optional extra, and neither is learning to relate. This is where counsellors and therapists can be useful because, above all, the task of therapy is to create a relationship within a safe and asexual environment. The relationship with the therapist ideally becomes the practice ground for relating skills, especially trust and control, which can then be applied in the real world.

Self-knowledge and Self-esteem

Of all the painful and disastrous effects of sexual abuse, perhaps the worst is the feeling of worthlessness and shame with which the victims are so often left. To abuse someone sexually is to use someone for your own pleasure and gratification without regard for the victim's feelings or needs. It is to use someone as an object, to deny them their personhood. No child can ever give 'consent' to sexual abuse, however much some abusers and some members of the judiciary might want to blame the child. No adult can deny responsibility for abusing a child by saying 'She led me on' or 'She wanted it' or 'She never objected'. The power imbalance between a child or a teenager and an adult man (or woman) is enormous and adults have a duty of responsibility towards a child not to abuse that position of power and trust.

Nevertheless, despite this, plenty of abused girls feel guilty, ashamed and responsible. They also feel made dirty and disgusting. In other words they take on the feelings and the responsibility that their abuser so often denies. The result of all this is very often a devastating sense of worthlessness. 'I feel', as many abused women have said to me, 'just like a piece of shit.'

To live your life day by day feeling that bad about yourself because you have been used by another person is a hard task. Many women try to escape the feeling by using drugs or alcohol. Others use food. The advantage of using an eating disorder in this situation is that you provide yourself with a whole way of thinking that gives meaning to your feeling of worthlessness. You feel fat and ugly and that makes sense of the devastating low self-esteem you feel.

The way out of this is not easy and not quick. It means first of all that you must get in touch with that abused child, see things from her point of view and recognise in a feeling way that what happened was not her fault and does not make her worthless or bad. Then you must begin to create and develop a clearer, firmer, stronger sense of self; for most women, this is a long, slow task. Women's work and women's lives are often seen as less important – think, for example, of the endless ongoing struggle to get equal pay for women. It is hard to transform your inner world when the outer world seems to echo so easily your own poor opinion of yourself. You need to begin to recognise your abilities and value them. One woman I worked with began to take her ability as an organiser seriously and gradually played an increasingly important role in a voluntary organisation. Another learned to value and enjoy her craft skills and took a relevant course leading to a recognised qualification. Another stopped saying she was useless as a mother and began to see that in some ways she was a good mother and in other ways she could develop and improve. In this process, these women gained confidence, learned more about themselves, started to feel that after all they were someone, not just a piece of shit but a person.

Even more important is to make sure that in your relationships and friendships and also at work you do not allow yourself to be treated badly and abusively. Too often when women have been abused they come to feel that being treated badly is normal and ordinary, and do not even consider that there is anything wrong. One of the rather powerful effects of therapy is that a woman is treated with respect. The therapist listens carefully to what is said, takes it seriously, wants to know about her experience and her thoughts about her life and its meaning. When a woman is not used to this kind of treatment it can provide a very strong contrast with the treatment she gets elsewhere. Sometimes this means she will leave a relationship that she begins to see is repeating the abuse of her childhood.

I would like to end this chapter with two case histories. The first is the story of a woman who had been abandoned as a child and brought up in care. Already, therefore, from a very young age she was a vulnerable child. Because of a series of misjudgements about whether she might eventually be able to return to her family, she was never offered for adoption and there was no long-term fostering arrangement made.

This girl, whom I will call Amanda (which means 'needing to be loved'), therefore grew up in a series of children's homes where she was both physically and sexually abused. This gross betrayal of a vulnerable child initially made her a withdrawn and lonely girl. At 16 she was required to leave the children's home and, with very little support, try and make her way in the world. The combined effect of all this was that she first developed anorexia and then bulimia as means of coping with an experience and an emotional history that was too much for her. When I met her she was very bulimic and not at all well as a result. It took a long time for the facts of her life to emerge. The connection between painful feelings which arose from her remembering her earlier life and the bulimia was made clear by the way that Amanda would start to talk about something she had remembered, then break off, saying that the only real problem was that she was overweight and that if only I would help her deal with that problem everything would be all right. Particularly because of the sexual abuse, Amanda was full of hatred for her body and herself, and underneath full of rage for those who had abused her. She found it hard to trust anyone even a little, with very good reason, and the abuse made the prospect of a relationship with a man or woman intolerably complicated and difficult. During the time I worked with her, Amanda was not able to give up the bulimia. She still needed it and was not yet ready to face the terrible disaster of her childhood without that protection. I felt she had done well to get as far as she did and she went on to get help from another source. What her story will illustrate perhaps, is the need and value of an eating disorder for a girl who has been abused, and the extent of the hard work that is necessary before she can give it up.

The other story is of a woman grossly and persistently abused by her father as a child, who developed anorexia. She married a man who was rather cold and withdrawn, whose attitude to sex was that it was a biological function, an urge in a man that had to be satisfied, but was of no more emotional significance than going to the toilet. And that is exactly how Sophie experienced his lovemaking, as if he went to the toilet inside her. However, having been accustomed to being abused, she did not even in a conscious way object until she began to do some work on herself because of her anorexia. She realised then both what a hideous trauma the abuse had been and how similar she felt her husband's lovemaking to be. She asked him to go with her to some couple counselling, which he did, but he was completely unable to understand what Sophie was complaining about. As he said repeatedly, he had no complaints; the only problem was Sophie's anorexia. To absorb the fact that Sophie did have complaints seemed beyond his power. As it became clearer over a period of many months that her husband was incapable of change and that her eating disorder had some connection with their sexual relationship, Sophie gradually came to the conclusion that she no longer wanted to be in the relationship. She felt strongly enough that she deserved and wanted something better to be able to leave and to begin to build a more satisfying and less anorexic life.

The wounds of sexual abuse can heal, and the disturbance they cause in ordinary living can be overcome. Often an eating disorder has been necessary as a means of survival, but if the underlying cause can be attended to and resolved then the eating disorder will no longer be necessary and can be discarded. I can't pretend that this process is usually quick or easy, but what it can do is enable you to become the person you have the power to be and free you from the need to hide from yourself.

The first step in being able to deal with a history of sexual abuse is to find the part of yourself that can be concerned for the child that was abused. There are a number of ways that you might develop this capacity inside yourself.

- You could write the story of your experiences in the third person; this often helps people to recognise what has been done to them.
- You could use a doll and talk to the doll as if it were you as an abused child.
- You could paint images of yourself and the abuser and see what feelings emerge.
- You could write a letter to the abuser telling him what you think of his behaviour.

There are more resources that you can use which are described in Chapter 12.

Chapter Ten

Me and My Body

We live in a world, in our western developed culture, that is extraordinarily conscious of appearance. We (women especially) have been taught over many years, perhaps beginning in the 1960s, to be constantly aware of how we look and to be hypercritical of our own appearance and that of other people. This 'lookist' society has become so familiar to us that we feel it is ordinary. We have created ideals for how women 'should' look and we are busily extending that system to men (see a magazine such as *Men's Health*, for instance). We talk about each other and make judgements on the basis of how we present ourselves physically. It used to be thought that women created their appearance for the benefit of men, but these days it seems as though women create their 'look' for other women and for themselves. The message seems to be: 'I am how I look.' The appearance of female celebrities is minutely analysed in magazines and on the internet and rarely praised. Instead, tiny presumed 'flaws' or 'mistakes' are noted and pointed out. We have been taught that how we look is the most important thing about us.

This system is at its most powerful for young women who can feel utterly destroyed if they think that how they look does not conform to what their social group demands or what they feel accurately represents them. It is likely that many of you reading this chapter will have felt unable to leave the house because your clothes, or your hair, or your shoes weren't right, or especially because you felt 'fat'. It is also likely that you are afraid of the reactions of others in your social group to the way you look; you may even have been bullied because of the way you look. It is known that young teenage girls particularly can be vicious to those who seem to be different or don't manage to match the group norms exactly. Those of you who truly are very overweight are especially vulnerable to this kind of treatment. One girl whose story was told in a BBC3 documentary, *The Thirty-Two Stone Teenager*, was bullied unmercifully because of her size. She described how she was locked in the classroom while the rest of the class went on a geography field trip. Another young woman I knew could only deal with being a size 18 by telling her friends that she had an illness which made her fat. Self-consciousness about your appearance can isolate you from your friends and spoil your social life.

Part of the reason for these social rules about how a young woman should look is that in our early teenage years we don't know who we are. We haven't lived long enough, done or learned enough to be able to construct a strong identity. We are still experimenting and learning and trying things out. Think about how common it is for teenagers to practise their signatures or change their hairstyles as ways of exploring who they are. Appearance can act as a kind of instant identity; if we conform to the rules of our social group then we probably feel a bit safer, not so exposed to all the puzzles and demands of growing up. It is probably the worry about not fitting in, being an outsider, that makes some young women so cruel to those who do not fit in. In addition, our appearance signals our gender identity – whether you are a man or a woman. Gender and sexuality are also huge issues for us all. Conforming to the norm of masculine or feminine appearance can make us feel safer, perhaps give us a hiding place while we figure out who we are.

The rejection of difference and strangeness is very common (at all ages) among those who feel challenged and insecure about their own identity. If I feel confident about who I am and how I look, I don't need to be critical and hostile to those who are different. It's as if I can say 'I feel fine about who I am and I'm happy for you to be who you are.' Unfortunately prejudice and hostility to others on the basis of skin colour, sexual orientation, religious affiliation, appearance or any number of other factors are exceedingly common among all human beings. We don't find it easy to be secure in ourselves and tolerant of others.

Body Image

So, the language of weight, shape and size has become one of the principle ways in which young women evaluate themselves and each other. This system is further driven by commercial interests. Clothes, make-up and beauty treatments are all sold by promising us that these products will make us more acceptable to ourselves and to others. The fashion industry presents images (air brushed and manipulated) that create an impossible ideal for most women. We can't all be tall and very slender. Indeed, the proportions of most fashion models are damagingly unhealthy and abnormal, but that doesn't prevent them from seeping right through our society: *Playboy* centrefolds, Barbie, average sizes for women, available clothes sizes. No wonder young women feel under enormous pressure to conform to these impossible norms and no wonder so many young women are driven by painful body dissatisfaction to try and torture themselves via disordered eating to a shape that they can bear to be.[1]

Stop and Think

What has your experience been of these kinds of pressures?

- Are you someone who has to be very sure that you look okay before you can leave the house?
- Could you describe the 'rules' of your social group for how you need to look?
- What happens if you (or someone else) doesn't conform?
- Does it seem correct to you to think of these rules as a way of creating an identity?
- Is that a way for you to feel safe when you are with other people?

These problems about body image can also have a damaging effect on sexual and intimate relationships. I have met women of all ages who felt so bad about the way they looked that they found it impossible to enjoy being with their partners. One woman in her forties comes to mind. Her name was Ruby; she had two teenage children and a husband who loved her deeply. He came to see me with Ruby because she found it so difficult to have a sexual relationship with him. She could not bear him to see her even partially undressed. She was obsessively private about her body and got no pleasure from sex because she could not forget her anxieties about her body. It became obvious as we talked that these problems had always been around for Ruby, but as she had got older and a bit heavier they had become worse, even though her husband had often tried to reassure her that he found her attractive and desirable. Now the marriage was in trouble because Ruby was in the process of ensuring that there was no sex between them. And interestingly, even though she hated being overweight, Ruby was steadily getting heavier because she used food to comfort herself.

It takes more than cultural pressures to create disordered eating, but before we talk about what else might be at work, let's think about other ways that we use to evaluate ourselves and each other. Before we go any further, have a go at the following exercise.

Stop and Think

Think of someone that you love very much. What is it about that person that makes them lovable to you? Make a list of at least three of those characteristics

My guess is that when you look at that list something will be absent from it – description of that person's appearance. It seems to me that we have two parallel and completely separate systems for evaluating people. With part of us we are judging and criticising someone's appearance and sometimes punishing or bullying that person for the way they look. With another part of ourselves we know perfectly well that what makes someone lovable, or a good friend, or someone we trust, has nothing to do with the way they look. We value qualities such as kindness, consideration, unselfishness, generosity, helpfulness, sense of humour, affection, intelligence. Our overvaluing of appearance is a superficial and (I would say) worthless way of knowing who to trust or who to love. If you agree with me, then perhaps you can begin to be more sceptical of those 'rules' and less concerned with following them. You – who you are – is vastly more important than how you look.

You can test this theory by thinking about someone you know who has a physical disability. If you have spent any time with that person you will have discovered that it doesn't take long to forget about the disability and to be conscious only of who that person really is. We really are so much more than the way we look.

One of the things that gets lost in our current obsession with appearance is that our bodies are functional – they are made to do something. Perhaps we can get an idea of the real value of our physicality by considering what it's like if your body doesn't work any more. The following quotation is from a series of articles written by Melanie Reid, a *Times* columnist who broke her neck and back after falling from a horse in April 2010:

> Nothing, take it from me, gives you a clearer perspective on society's obsession with physical desirability than a date with spinal paralysis, although I imagine that suffering from other terrible illnesses must do the same. When one is fighting for one's life or physical identity . . . there is something profoundly alienating about a world that increasingly judges people solely by their ever-readiness and suitability for sex. . . . When something as catastrophic as paralysis strikes, it completely alters your view . . . of what matters in life. And probably top of the What No Longer Matters list are the various shallow insanities of the fashion and beauty industry and our obsession with being thin.
>
> — Melanie Reid, Spinal Column, *Times*, 10 July 2010

Self-concept

But let's return to the subject of you and your body and what that has to do with disordered eating. I was saying that young women especially, are under enormous pressure to conform to norms of appearance which are observed by their social group and that these pressures are part of what can lie behind disordered eating. But if that were all it took to create disordered eating the entire female population (and maybe a good number of the males) would be suffering. However common disordered eating is, it's not that common. So what else is going on?

You'll remember that all the way through this book I've been returning to the theme of attachment. What does your attachment history have to do with your anxieties about your appearance and your body? Well, we know that secure attachment helps us develop a good sense of who we are and good self-esteem. If you live in a household where you feel loved and appreciated for yourself, your personality, your essential self, then you will very likely grow up feeling good about yourself and maybe less bothered about what other people think of you. If, on the other hand, you have been led to believe that you are not what your parents or caregivers want, and maybe told that you were stupid or lazy or just a nuisance, then it will be much more difficult for you to believe that you are okay.

Nowadays that sense of yourself is called self-concept or self-esteem and we know that it can vary for different parts of your life or your functioning. So, for instance, you may feel fine about how you do your schoolwork, but rubbish about the way you look. You may feel good about yourself as a friend, but miserable about your weight. Try the following exercise. Look at the different areas that I have identified and score yourself for how you think you manage in each of them. For instance, if you feel good about yourself in relation to your education give yourself 8 or 9 or 10 out of 10, but if that's a part of your life that makes you feel embarrassed or inadequate or despairing, give yourself a 2 or a 3 or a 4. Add extra sections if you think I've missed out something that's important for you.

Part of your life	Score
Education	
Appearance/weight	
As a friend	
As a son/daughter	
As a (step)parent	
As a partner	
Money	
Exercise	
Work	
?	
?	

Most people find that there are considerable differences in their scores for the different parts. For instance, you might feel very good about yourself in relation to work and not nearly so good in relation to how you manage your money. It's likely that for you appearance will be a low score; it very often is for people with disordered eating. That's not necessarily because your appearance is all that different from other people, but because you have focused on appearance as a way of judging yourself, or of repeating the negative judgements that other people have made of you. You have probably also used your negative feelings about your appearance to create a blanket judgement of yourself, forgetting all the other bits of you that probably function quite well.

So let's try and identify some of the experiences in the past that might have contributed to the way you feel about your body now. Let's begin by thinking about your life up to the age of 11 or 12. I remember very well a story I was told about one woman whose mother had her on a diet from as long as she could remember so that she had felt 'wrong' in her body all her life. Do you have that sort of experience?

Stop and Think

– Do you have any memories of your family's reactions to your size, shape or appearance when you were a child?

– Were those comments positive and admiring?

– Do you think that your caregivers liked and enjoyed the way you looked or were they critical or even hostile?

– Find a photograph from that time of your life and see if the way you look in that photograph corresponds to the way you felt.

School is an important influence on our feelings about our bodies, especially since children are aware of their appearance at earlier and earlier ages. Many clients have told me they were embarrassed about their bodies while they were still in primary school, especially if they couldn't run as fast as other children or couldn't balance or play games as skilfully.

Stop and Think

What do you remember from primary school about physical activity? Think first about organised activities – sports days, gym lessons or equivalent, e.g. music and movement, dancing, organised games, e.g. relay races. Write down some key words relating to these memories.

Then think about informal physical activity, e.g. games of chase or football in the playground, skipping, hopscotch, etc. What are your memories about participating or not in these sorts of activities? Do you have memories of teachers' reactions, or the reactions of other children, to your physicality. Write down some key words.

If your early experience has been good you are likely to feel pretty secure about your appearance and your physicality at around the age of 12, which is just as well because the changes of puberty can be very hard to manage. They seem to be particularly hard for girls who would sometimes like to retain a pre-pubertal body shape, whereas for boys the increase in size and development of pubic hair, etc. is generally a cause of satisfaction. If you are entering this phase of your development already feeling bad about how you look, teenage years can be truly awful. Ideally, you need a home base that feels safe where the changes are celebrated and accepted as part of an entirely natural and desirable development, and a group of friends who will support each other in coming to terms with the weird process of growing into an adult body. But I have heard often about thoughtless comments from caregivers such as 'Getting a bit tubby, aren't you?' and about humiliation at school around being selected for teams, or mocked for your appearance.

Stop and Think

 What are your memories of your family's reaction to
your adolescent physicality? Was it possible to discuss
your feelings about your changing body and rely on a
sympathetic hearing? Were these matters ever discussed
or mentioned? Were you mocked or criticised at home
for your appearance? Write down some key words.

What about school? Did you get support from
your friends around the physical changes or were you
mocked or bullied about your appearance?

Were you able to feel good about your body through
sport of any kind, or was that a part of your life which
contributed to your unhappiness. Was there any area of
activity (playing in a band/dancing, engaging in outdoor
activities such as camping/climbing; learning a skill such
as riding/martial arts) where you did feel good about
what you could do?

Write down some key words for important memories

These memories and experiences may well have taught
you how to dislike your body and it is highly likely that you
have repeated these judgements to yourself ever since. Maybe
they are so familiar to you that you don't pause to consider
whether they are true, important or useful. Maybe you use
them like a stick to beat yourself with. The unfortunate effect
of reinforcing someone else's opinion of the way you look is
that you become unable to think your own thoughts, in fact
you probably think they are your own thoughts. Then in turn
those thoughts will have an effect and since you are a person
who has problems with food, they probably affect your eating
behaviour. So it very likely goes like this:

Someone else's opinion (real or imagined) of how
you look, or your own judgement of yourself

↓

Makes you feel bad, ugly, worthless, disgusting, etc.

↓

So you start to tell yourself what a
loathsome, horrible sight you are

↓

Which makes you feel even worse

↓

And so in order to escape from these
horrible thoughts and feelings

↓

You soothe yourself with food

↓

Either you eat or binge or you
vow to deny yourself food

↓

So your disordered eating is worse and you
still feed bad, or even worse about yourself.

You need to be able to use your grown-up, rational mind to control those feelings, to challenge them and to refuse to be controlled by old stories and repetitive thoughts. Here are some other possibilities:

- I don't care what he/she thinks.
- I can accept the way I am.
- What right has he/she to judge me?
- How do I know what they are thinking?
- I don't need to keep repeating these old stories to myself.
- I will not let worry about my appearance spoil my life.

There is much more that will be useful to you in an excellent book called the *Body Image Workshop* by Thomas Cash,[2] which has all sorts of really good exercises to help you change your way of thinking about yourself.

Wordless Messenger

Let's apply these ideas to disordered eating and ask whether it could be true that you are using food and its effect on your body as a wordless messenger of what is going on with you? We know that quite ordinary and well-understood emotional states such as anxiety or grief frequently produce altered eating behaviour. So what else might you be trying to express with your body? All through this book I have been suggesting that disordered eating is a response to all sorts of experiences and circumstances that produce feelings which seem unmanageable. Food and preoccupation with weight, shape and size are ways of expressing, coping with, avoiding, diverting from or otherwise reacting to those underlying issues. Using your body like that protects from all sorts of things: sex, intimacy, other people's demands, change, adult responsibility. At the same time it signals distress, suffering, pain and helplessness.

I think this is why it is so difficult to surrender all forms of disordered eating. If you give it up, how will you be able to convey your pain? I once had a client who said exactly that to me. She had been on the receiving end of seriously abusive treatment from both her parents. She said, 'If I get better from my eating disorder, then everyone will think that there was nothing wrong with my childhood and my parents will be able to pretend that nothing ever happened.' Her eating disorder was a living message of her pain and intended as a permanent reproach to her parents. It was so important for this woman to tell this story with her body that she ignored the fact that in the process she was destroying her own future and her own life.

Stop and Think

 If your body could speak, what would it say? What is the message that you are trying to convey with your disordered eating?

This way of thinking about disordered eating is very similar to the way that self-harm expresses distress via a use of the body. It's not too difficult to see disordered eating as a form of self-harm. There's an obvious urgent need to find an alternative way of exploring what's going on with you. The opposite of hating and harming our bodies is to love and nurture them. I recommend an excellent book by Astrid Longhurst called *Body Confidence*[3]. Astrid is a big woman who has had terrible struggles with her body image, but has won through to accepting and even liking and loving her body. She has plenty of ideas about how to change the currency of loathing and harming ourselves to enjoying and nurturing ourselves. She proposes a 'Body Journey' to help you achieve body confidence and let go of the self-hatred that is so self-limiting.

> Life is far too short to be spent in self-loathing rejecting the person you are and the body you have. The minutes are ticking by as we worry about all of our shortcomings instead of celebrating our most positive strengths and abilities. I never used to notice how beautiful the day was, because I was too busy noticing how ugly I thought I was. I was never fully in touch with my life because I was so out of touch with myself. When you deny and dislike the person you are then your entire world centres around this. I made excuses not to go to parties; I failed to show up to go swimming or horseriding. I backed out of going away on holiday with friends and later on in my twenties I found reasons not to get involved in relationships or have sex. The ridiculous thing was that underneath it all I desperately wanted to experience all those things but felt unworthy of allowing my body or myself that pleasure.
> — Astrid Longhurst, *Body Confidence*, 2003

Stop and Think

 Try these exercises as a way of creating a different way of thinking about your body:

- What difference would it make to your life if you really loved your body?
- How would it change the way you dress and present yourself?
- How would it change the way you look after yourself?
- How would it change your relationships and friendships?

Chapter Eleven
Men and Disordered Eating

"In recent years, the notion that disordered eating is simply a female problem has become somewhat incongruent with the clear pressures now on men to manage weight or acquire and maintain idealised physiques….These pressures are part of a complex array of factors pointing to the likelihood of an increased number of men encountering difficulties with eating."

—Ewan Gillon, in *Eating Disorders in Men*, 2005[1]

"In a population based survey of American households. . . . we found a surprisingly high proportion of men with anorexia nervosa and bulimia nervosa (representing approximately one fourth of cases of each of these disorders)."

—Hudson et al., *Biological Psychiatry*, 2007[2]

Much of what has been said in the previous ten chapters may well have been relevant to men reading this book. It is not only women who have to manage the problems of making the transition from adolescent to adult or surviving difficult or abusive beginnings. Attachment history is just as relevant to men as to women and men as well as women need to be able to self-soothe and find others for support and love. Having said that, there do seem to be some features of male disordered eating that are different from women's experience and ways of thinking. In this chapter I will try and explore what they are.

Let's begin, though, with an attempt to estimate how common eating disorders are in men. The short answer is, nobody really knows. The old answer is that for every ten women coming into treatment, there was one man. Quite a number of bits of evidence seem to suggest that the actual figure might be quite a lot higher. The evidence from Hudson et al. quoted at the beginning of this chapter suggests that in the USA as many as one in four cases might be male. There is a strong suspicion that the popular view of eating disorders as a 'woman's disease' may make it very difficult for men to seek treatment, or even to have their difficulties recognised by the medical profession. Whenever there is publicity about males with eating disorders, the numbers of those presenting themselves for treatment increases. As far as obesity is concerned, the prevalence in the UK is virtually identical to that in women, somewhere about 25 per cent. How many of them are emotional eaters is unknown, although it is known that much male obesity is connected with alcohol consumption as well as overeating. Many obese women are quite capable of identifying their eating as emotionally driven. I am not sure that would be quite so easy for men, who are rarely expected to talk as freely about feelings or emotional experience.

Eddie's Story

Eddie was a consulting engineer who earned his living with contracts to various manufacturers. His job was to visit engineering works and deal with problems in the manufacturing process. It was stimulating work, often demanding both physically and intellectually. Eddie loved it and was good at it. In his spare time he was a keen rugby player, strong and fit, and an enthusiastic participant in the rugby club after-match celebrations. He was full of life and energy, great company and popular with his rugby-playing friends.

However, engineering works are dangerous places, especially where there are defective machines. On one job Eddie injured the top of his foot on a protruding piece of metal. Although he was wearing boots, the metal ripped through the leather and gashed his foot. The first aid team at the works were a bit concerned about the wound and suggested that Eddie went to the emergency department at the local hospital, but Eddie was keen to finish the job and get back home for the weekend. He assured the team that the injury was nothing serious and he would seek further help if it caused him any bother. Ten days later Eddie was at work feeling very strange. He was having a coffee break when one of his colleagues asked him if he had been drinking, 'You're acting strange, Eddie. Are you drunk?' Another friend joined in, 'Yeah, Eddie, what's wrong, and what's that weird smell – like acetone?' When Eddie showed them his foot, the friends were horrified and immediately called an ambulance. Within hours Eddie was in the operating theatre having his gangrenous foot and leg amputated.

In the space of a day Eddie's life altered beyond recognition. Instead of being a fit active sportsman, he was now in a wheelchair and would never play rugby again. He lost his job and his livelihood – there were no jobs in his profession for disabled men. He was also faced with the prospect of a long and painful rehabilitation, learning to use a prosthetic leg and attempting to regain mobility. Not surprisingly, Eddie became deeply depressed. There was no psychological help offered to enable him to negotiate this desperate transition, so Eddie self-medicated with food and alcohol. In the space of a few months he began a process of weight gain that made his remobilising ever more unlikely and confined him unwillingly and uncomfortably to a wheelchair.

Eventually, as he became ever heavier, he was referred by his GP to a weight loss programme. This programme was unusual in that it asked participants to think about the causes and meaning of their overweight. Little by little Eddie began to put together the story of his injury and the amputation with his radical change of circumstances and his terrible anger and disappointment with his disability. He began to see that he had been trying to help himself manage that change with his eating and drinking and that he needed to come to terms with his situation and find a new way to lead his life. He decided that he would be most useful helping other disabled people manage their situations, and over time trained and worked in that occupation. With these realisations came a change in his eating behaviour. His resentment at being required to lose weight was replaced by a more matter of fact recognition of the value of being more mobile. His resolution was to reduce from 165 kilos to 115 kilos, the weight he had been when he lost his leg. It seemed that after a long detour he was ready to resume life where it had been interrupted. Nowadays, he says that his recovery would have been greatly assisted by some psychological help, but that he has got to the point of accepting his body and no longer feels the need to self-medicate with food and drink.

Eddie's disastrous experience arose partly from his failure to seek medical help soon enough. It is known that men in the UK consult GPs less often than women.[3] They are less likely to report health worries and less likely to be given health advice. In an obesity service that I ran in a primary care trust (PCT) only about 20 per cent of referrals were for men. Yet there are as many obese men as women. Because male obesity is abdominal, it is more dangerous than female obesity around the hips and thighs.

Eddie's failure to adapt to his new situation was also because men are much less likely to be offered psychological help or to accept it. Our culture still expects men to be strong and unemotional (although women frequently complain about exactly that) and many men expect it of themselves. Vulnerability or distress are experienced as weakness, or being like a woman – the ultimate threat to a man's sense of himself. Feelings get translated into behaviour and for some men that behaviour is overeating. Many women can use their female friends and relations for emotional support; it is common for women to meet and talk about their emotional experience and their feelings. Men rarely have this kind of emotional support, although some men can use their partners in this way.

Stop and Think

- Does it seem true for you that feelings get translated into eating behaviour?
- Do you think that you are less likely than your female friends to discuss your feelings or your emotional experience?
- Does the expression of upset or distress make you feel too vulnerable?

Male Body Image

Traditionally, the body has not been the site of men's identity and conflicts as it has for women. Men have invested much more heavily in work and achievement, sometimes as measured by money. In consequence, dieting and body dissatisfaction have not exercised the same kind of pressures on men as they have on women. However, over the past 20 years or so this has been changing. The change seems to have worked in two directions and has been driven by images in the media. One strand has been the use of images of males with adolescent bodies – thin, with a lack of muscle development and an appearance of weakness, 'heroin chic' as it is sometimes known. The other strand has been the popularisation of heavily muscled bodies, often where the upper body is overdeveloped and the abdominal muscles form a 'six pack'. The first set of images is usually found in advertisements for luxury goods, but the second is increasingly visible in a range of settings, including popular magazines such as *Men's Health*. They are also visible in the shape of action toys for boys. Just as Barbie has presented a grossly distorted image of the female body to girls, so Action Man does the same for boys.[4] There is a further cultural vulnerability to body dissatisfaction for homosexual men who are often more body conscious than heterosexual men. Approximately 20 per cent of men with eating disorders are gay.[5]

As well as the familiar categories of eating disorder, men seem to suffer from a specific disorder, perhaps media led, known variously as muscle dysmorphia, bigarexia or reverse anorexia. In this condition, a man wishes to develop a highly muscled body but feels that his body is never big enough. This leads to over-exercise combined with a reduction in fat and carbohydrate in the diet, an increase in protein and sometimes the use of protein supplements or anabolic steroids.[6]

Just as women with body image problems are found in the 'thin' professions such as modelling, dancing, gymnastics, etc., so the same seems to be true of men. There are reports of eating disorders in male sports such as wrestling and cycling.

Stop and Think

How relevant are media images of males to you? Do you find yourself comparing yourself to them?

It is likely that participation in these activities is attractive to those who value the body shape that the activity requires.

However, sport is in general much more interesting to men than to women, both as spectators and as participants. Probably it offers opportunities for the competition and achievement that are so important to men. Success in sport offers men the kind of improvement of self-esteem and identity that meeting social norms for appearance gives women. For most men, this involvement in sport is unproblematic, but when sport has to compensate for anxieties in other parts of a man's life, then it means too much.

James's Story

James was 15 and a keen cricketer. He had loved cricket since he was a small boy and went to a school where he had steadily moved up through the teams and was playing for junior teams at the local cricket club and for his county. Cricket also compensated to some extent for James's distress at his father's diagnosis of cancer. James's mother had been distraught at the diagnosis, so James had done his best to comfort her and to put his own feelings to one side. As James's father grew more and more unwell, James applied himself to cricket with more and more focus. When he was practising and playing he could forget how things were at home. A passing comment by his coach that he could perhaps do with losing a few pounds set him on a course of dieting and weight loss. Within four months he had lost half a stone, even though he was still growing. Positive comments from the coach reinforced his determination to continue his steadily more restrictive diet. This story might have had very serious consequences, but fortunately the school was aware of James's father's illness. The pastoral care staff noticed his weight loss, his progressively poorer concentration in class and his general appearance of unhappiness. His tutor had already won James's trust and liking, so it was not too difficult for him to engage James in discussion about what was going on with him. The fact that the tutor was also a keen follower of cricket created an easy way for them to relate. James was able to confide his desperate anxieties about his father and mother and express some of his fears for the future. As James began to allow himself to be more aware of his feelings, he was encouraged by his tutor to talk to his parents. He then discovered how worried they had been about him and how helpless they had felt in the face of his obsession with cricket and his weight loss. The three of them were able to come much closer and re-establish communication. They were able to talk together about James's father's illness and even dare to think about the possibility that he might die. James's mother recognised her need for proper support outside the family and as a result was more able to support James. Within eight months James's weight was back to normal and the friends who had slipped away as he became more and more strange started to hang out with him again. He was nervous about starting back to cricket, but the coach was very keen to have him back, and this time was determined to keep a close eye on him.

Overweight boys suffer humiliation and bullying from their peer group. Most will try and maintain a veneer of good humour, if for no other reason than fear of even worse

Stop and Think

Do you recognise the obsessionalism and perfectionism that are evident from James's story? Think back to when those traits began to be evident; can you see what might have triggered your preoccupation? Does it seem likely to you that it might have been a coping mechanism in response to some life circumstance?

treatment, but will later acknowledge the tremendous shame induced by this behaviour. Abuse of this kind is extremely destructive of self-esteem and leads to self-loathing. It often erodes the confidence to engage in the ordinary processes of forming sexual relationships and training and education.

Matt's Story

Matt grew up as the only child of a single mother. Her need to earn a living meant that Matt was often alone at home and passed the time watching television or playing computer games. He consoled himself for his loneliness by eating the snacks his mother provided to keep him going until she got back from work. By the age of ten he was already significantly overweight and was beginning to be teased at school. The teasing made him unwilling to play football with his mates or even to muck about on his bike with other lads. The reduction in his activity was compounded when he went to secondary school, leaving the relative safety of his small primary school. He was repeatedly bullied by other boys, called names and mocked for his inability to run as fast as they could. A favourite game was to take his schoolbag and run off with it and then dump it somewhere that Matt could not easily reach. The compulsory physical education (PE) and games lessons were a form of torture. PE staff seemed to have no strategies at all to deal with him in a way that took account of his overweight.

By the time Matt was in the second year of his secondary education he was already beginning to truant. The less time he spent at school, the more difficult it was to return. For a while he managed a little better in a unit for youngsters who for all sorts of reasons found it difficult to be in the main stream. At least the teachers there enforced a tolerance of difference from all pupils. However, Matt gradually slipped further and further out of education. By the time he was 15 he was hardly at school and the attendance officers seemed to have given up on him. Despite his desperately poor self-esteem, and urged on by his mother, Matt managed to get himself a job in a warehouse. Earning a wage made him feel a bit better, and although his workmates teased him he did not suffer the kind of malice he had experienced at school. A perceptive manager encouraged Matt to do some training to become a fork-lift driver and he settled into a manageable routine. However, his obesity had significantly limited his social and emotional development. He still lived at home

Stop and Think

Do you recognise any of this story? Which bits of it do you identify with? How do you think you could make a better ending than the one that is reported here? What do you think would have made it possible for Matt to surrender his use of food for companionship and comfort?

with his mother and had never had an intimate or sexual relationship. He was aware that he continued to compensate for his frustrations and disappointments by eating and that in turn he continued to feel enormous shame about his size.

Change in eating behaviour for men is often made even more difficult by cultural factors. What is eaten in a family is usually managed by women; men can often feel embarrassed by wanting to change their eating behaviour. After all, real men don't eat quiche (still less salad).

Steve's Story

Steve had suffered a mild heart attack, but had been told by the consultant that unless he changed his diet and lost weight he would be back again within two years with a much more serious heart attack. He was referred to a programme of cardiac rehabilitation. For three months he was invited to attend once a week at a session where he and a group of men and a few women were given a class about improving their diet and then half an hour of exercise. Steve hated the sessions and would not have continued had he not been pressured to do so by his wife. He felt humiliated by the process of being instructed about what he should eat by 'a girl', as he said. The exercise was acutely embarrassing, not least because Steve was very unfit and poorly co-ordinated and felt a total fool in an exercise class. The whole process seemed to him to undermine his male pride. The recommendations to eat fruit and vegetables in greater quantities than Steve had ever done before also felt like a demand to eat 'women's food'. The weekly weighing similarly felt like a female activity. He stuck out the classes for two months, but then point blank refused to return. Unfortunately, he was never able to articulate the real reason for his reluctance to engage with his rehabilitation; he became yet another dropout who appeared not to be able to recognise his own best interests.

However, one thing was helpful to Steve in the ideas he heard at the class. The 'girl' had asked the class to consider what kind of an example they were giving their children by their eating behaviour. Steve had a son, a boy of ten called Jake, with whom he shared an interest in football and cars. These interests had previously been expressed by sitting watching television together; Steve began to see that he was teaching his son habits that would inevitably lead to him becoming overweight. At the same time he noticed how his son declared that he liked the food his father liked: sausages, pork pies, bacon and egg sandwiches. Steve started to take responsibility for the lessons his son was learning. Slowly and steadily, for his son's sake, he began to improve his diet and

Stop and Think

- Have you been able to find a way of addressing your eating behaviour in a way that feels congruent with you as a man?
- If you were planning a course to help you change, what would it look like?
- How specifically would you address the needs of men in a group setting?
- What sorts of approach would strengthen your self-esteem and male pride?
- Would it help to have some competitive element with other men?
- Can you apply some of these ideas to yourself and your wish to change?[7]

become more active. He enjoyed a kick about in the park and he discovered that bananas and tangerines actually tasted quite good and were easy to eat. He couldn't get enthusiastic about salad, but he steered Jake away from fish and chips and made Saturday the night when the boys, Steve and Jake, made dinner for the girls, no fry-ups allowed.

Part III

Chapter Twelve

Resources

Finding Professional Help

There are different sorts of professionals who deal with psychological problems. Most people's journey to find help for any kind of disordered eating starts with their GP. He or she is unlikely to have any specialist knowledge of the subject and will evaluate your need for referral to other professionals. Mostly your GP will attempt to evaluate the seriousness of your condition over time. Often the next stop will be with a dietician or nutritionist. If that does not prove helpful, or if your GP considers your condition to be primarily psychological, you may be referred to the in-house, non-specialist counselling service. Some counsellors are well informed about eating disorders but many are not, and in most cases you will be given no more than about six sessions of counselling. If you then want further help you need to go back to your GP and ask him to refer you to a specialist service. This can be a difficult and slow process. Often GPs will first refer you to community mental health services for an assessment. This is where the vexed question of diagnosis can play a part. If you are not diagnosable with an eating disorder, or if you are not considered particularly unwell, you may be offered support via a community mental health worker rather than a referral to specialist services. These workers may also not have any specialist knowledge of eating disorders. If you are referred to a specialist service, you may find you have a considerable further wait for an appointment. Again you will be assessed, and again if you are not considered diagnosable or sufficiently unwell you will not be offered treatment. If you become really unwell, especially with anorexia, you may be referred to a specialist hospital unit where you will be seen by a psychiatrist. Psychiatrists are doctors who are trained in the administration of drugs for psychological conditions. Sometimes they have had additional therapy training, but by no means always. Specialist eating disorder psychiatrists will have a great deal of experience in working with this client group and usually will have responsibility for the overall management of an individual's treatment as an outpatient or, in a very limited number of cases, as an inpatient.

This can be a difficult and discouraging journey. B-eat, the UK eating disorders charity, has repeatedly identified and lobbied to improve the provision of services for eating disorders. There is a 'post code lottery' with provision in some areas of the UK much better than others.

If you feel that you want help in sorting out the psychological issues which underlie your disordered eating, you can access counselling directly via the various websites of counselling associations. These will describe the training and theoretical orientation of the therapist and will indicate whether he or she has specific competence in working with eating disorders. No/low cost agencies are also listed (search by area). A key source of information is the website of the British Association for Counselling and Psychotherapy – by far the largest of the therapy associations: http://www.bacp.co.uk/. It operates an accreditation scheme for more experienced therapists. The site also has a FAQs section which will guide you in choosing who to contact.

Counselling Directory is another well-respected site: http://www.counselling-directory.org.uk/.

Accredited cognitive behavioural therapy (CBT) therapists can be found at http://cbtregisteruk.com/.

In choosing a therapist in any setting, bear in mind that you are the consumer. Much research on the efficacy of counselling concludes that the relationship with the counsellor is one of the most important factors in whether it will be successful (the other most significant factor is whether you are ready to work on your difficulties). You need to feel that you could like and trust this person. Many researchers think that these criteria are more important in recovery than the theoretical orientation of the therapist. Some research shows that in practice, whatever their label, successful therapists create warm and friendly relationships with their clients and integrate a range of strategies into their treatments.

Guidelines for the Non-professional Helper

If you are willing to take on the role of a companion or buddy to a person whose eating is disordered who wants to work through this book, you need to think first about what that role implies before committing yourself to it.

Let's Start with What You are not!

You are not a specialist in disordered eating, either from a medical or a psychological point of view. You need to be able to recognise the limits of your competence and if you feel that you are out of your depth to refer to other people – for instance, a GP or counselling agency. You also need to agree with your 'client', who I will call Polly for ease of reference, that if you feel that what she says is causing you real concern, or if you are afraid for her emotional or physical welfare, that she will agree to seek alternative additional help.

Should You Give Advice?

Well, no. Your job is to help Polly find her own good advice. A person with disordered eating almost always knows what would be good for her in terms of food. She also probably has a pretty fair idea of what would be best in other areas of her life, if she has time and space and a concerned listener (you) to help her work it out. However, Polly has no confidence in her own judgement and her self-esteem is shockingly poor, so she doesn't believe she can figure it out. But she can.

Should You Talk about Yourself and Your Eating Behaviour?

Probably not. The space you have created is for Polly and although she may ask you about yourself, that might well be because she is worried about taking the space herself. She might find it easier to listen to you than to talk about herself, but the point of your meetings is for her to reflect on her progress through this book.

Should You Ask Questions?

Mostly not, but it sometimes helps to use prompts, such as: 'What happened then?'; How did you feel when he said that? What do you think she meant?' Your questions should enable Polly to expand on what she is saying and to think about it further. Beware of opening new subjects or asking for a lot of detailed information. Let Polly be the judge of where the conversation should go.

Should We Meet Regularly?

If you have agreed together to work your way through this book, then I think regular meetings are a good idea. Probably not more than once a week, but not at very long intervals either, because you will lose momentum. But it's a good idea to discuss these things at the very beginning, so that you both know what you are taking on. You need to agree how long your meetings will last. There's nothing wrong with short meetings (of say 15 minutes) if that's all the time you have, but this won't give you time to explore anything in much detail. Difficult subjects and memories need more time than that, but there's a useful convention that an hour is long enough for these sorts of conversations. You also need to agree what you are going to discuss at the next meeting, so that both of you have time to read the relevant bit of the book and think about it.

Where should We Meet?

The meeting place should preferably be somewhere that is private and a space that feels fairly neutral; somewhere quiet, where you won't be interrupted; somewhere where you both feel safe.

Further Reading

There is an excellent book by John McLeod (2007) *Counselling Skill*, Maidenhead, Open University Press, explicitly written for professionals (teacher, nurse, social worker, lawyer, etc.) who find themselves functioning in a counselling role. It maps out very clearly how 'embedded counselling', as McLeod calls it, can work.

Diagnosis of Eating Disorders

There are two versions of these standards, one is called *DSM IV* (shortly to be replaced by *DSM V*). It is the textbook for the American Psychiatric Association which uses it to diagnose all sorts of emotional conditions and mental illnesses. The other is called *ICD-10* and is the World Health Organisation's equivalent. In the UK it is mostly *DSM* that is used, but their descriptions of eating disorders are very similar.

There are several websites which give you these definitions:

- http://www.b-eat.co.uk/ is the website of the Eating Disorders Association, now known as B-eat, the largest UK charity dealing with these issues.
- http://www.medic.ca/ puts the information in an accessible form.
- http://www.nationaleatingdisorders.org/ is an excellent website.

Treatment of Disordered Eating

The National Institute of Health and Clinical Excellence (NICE) is a government agency which has as its responsibility the evaluation of treatments for medical conditions. Its conclusions are published as guidelines and updated periodically. Its reports can be accessed at http://www.nice.org.uk

and are available to download or to buy in hard copy. There are longer and shorter versions of the reports, some written for health professionals and some for the public. The principal report on eating disorders is called *Core Interventions in the Treatment and Management of Anorexia Nervosa, Bulimia Nervosa and Related Eating Disorders* (2004).

The equivalent guideline for obesity is called *Obesity: The Prevention, Identification, Assessment and Management of Overweight and Obesity in Adults and Children* (2006), which gives minimum attention to psychological issues (despite the copious literature on the subject) in the development of obesity.

Guidelines are developed via the consideration of published research on treatments, according to a formula known as the 'hierarchy of evidence' which prefers research carried out according to specific conventions. There is debate as to whether these conventions are appropriate for researching psychological conditions, but the exponents of cognitive behaviour therapy (CBT) have been far more energetic than those of other treatments in carrying out research of that kind. Not surprisingly, the NICE guidelines have determined that CBT is the best evidenced treatment for disordered eating of all kinds (although there is less certainty in the guidelines about treatment for anorexia for which family therapy is recommended). There are many therapists (among whom I number) who are less than convinced by the idea of CBT as the only suitable treatment. Cognitive therapies have no interest in why the eating behaviour developed in the first place, but focus on changing the current thought patterns and behaviour. Of course, these are crucial elements in recovery; there is no recovery without them. In addition, it is clear that we do manage our feelings via our thoughts. However, many people distressed by their eating behaviour want to understand where it comes from and want to tell their story and explore their feelings. CBT also depends absolutely on the capacity of the patient/client to identify feeling and thoughts in relation to their eating behaviour/ body image, and by no means all of them are, at least initially, ready to do this.

My preference is for a pluralist approach such as that described by Cooper and McLeod (2010) in *Pluralistic Counselling and Psychotherapy*, where the client's readiness, capacity and way of working are taken into account and where a combination of approaches can be used, as seems appropriate. I want the freedom to explore feelings, thoughts, memories, fantasies, dreams, stories, hopes, fears – anything that is important to the client. There is fierce debate on this subject within the therapy world, so you need to think hard about the style of therapy that would suit you before committing yourself. You also need to see how you get on with a therapist of any persuasion (as indicated above). What follows is an indication of some of the range of approaches and books that use them.

Cognitive Behaviour Therapy

The principle research team in the UK developing CBT treatments for eating disorders is led by Professor Christopher Fairburn in Oxford. He is a distinguished researcher of many years experience. The most recent book which expounds his approach is *Cognitive Behaviour Therapy for Eating Disorders* (2008). It's a book for clinicians but is written in a very accessible style. His central idea is that all disordered eating is distinguished by 'the over-valuation of weight and shape and their control' (Fairburn, 2008, 12). The book sets out to change this way of thinking in clients and offers guidelines for implementing his approach. As you will see, this is a radically different way of thinking from the one employed in this book.

Fairburn has also written a self-help book, *Overcoming Binge Eating* (1995), which similarly focuses on how to change thinking and behaviour about eating and offers a programme for how to go about it.

Another self-help book using the CBT approach is by Peter Cooper – *Bulimia Nervosa and Binge Eating: A Self-help Guide Using Cognitive Behavioural Techniques* (2009).

Solution Focused Therapy

Problem solving (i.e. what do you do when it all goes wrong) is a key part of CBT, but there is also a therapy which uses this approach on its own. The key book is by Frederike Jacob (2001) *Solution Focused Recovery from Eating Distress*. Again, this approach is explicitly not interested in the question of how you came to have disordered eating in the first place, but has some useful strategies for moving on. You may have to get in touch with the author to get the book – look her up on the internet.

Transactional Analysis

Transactional analysis was developed in the 1960s by Eric Berne and popularised by Thomas Harris in *I'm OK – You're OK*. It's a style of therapy which bridges the cognitive and more meaning seeking therapies, and in my experience is sometimes more readily understood and put into use by clients than CBT. In the same way it involves listening to the conversation you are having with yourself, but talks about it in terms of three main voices – parent, adult and child. Many of my clients have been able to identify the critical parent voice and the upset/angry child voice and have worked to find the grown-up, rational, soothing voice. There isn't a TA book specifically on disordered eating, but Kathy Leach (2006) *The Overweight Patient: A Psychological Approach to Understanding and Working with Obesity*, again written for the counsellor but quite accessible, will give you an idea of how TA could be applied to other forms of disordered eating. In any case, I think it's worth reading *I'm OK – You're OK* as a way into being more aware of your internal conversation.

Family Therapy

In recent years much more attention has been paid to how families respond to eating disorders, especially anorexia (but very little to how they may engender them). Much of this work has gone on at the Maudsley Hospital in South London and has resulted in a practical book for families: Janet Treasure et al. (2007) *Skills Based Learning for Caring for a Loved One with an Eating Disorder: The New Maudsley Method*.

A more technical description from the same stable comes from James Lock et al. (2002) *Treatment Manual for Anorexia Nervosa: A Family-based Approach*.

Arts Therapies

The difficulty in identifying and talking about feelings that has been noted in this book has given rise to the use of arts therapies for disordered eating. An older but valuable book is by Lynne Hornyak and Ellen Baker (1989), *Experiential Therapies for Eating Disorders*. This gives many examples of how arts therapies of all kinds can be used to facilitate the expression of feelings and enable reflection.

Another book along the same lines is by Ditty Dokter (1994) *Arts Therapies and Clients with Eating Disorders.*

In *Art Therapy and Eating Disorders: The Self as Significant Form*, Mury Rabin (2003) is particularly concerned with facilitating the development of better body image and sense of self.

Integrative Therapy

You'll have gathered by now that I consider a therapy that uses a range of approaches to disordered eating the most useful way of proceeding. Kathryn Zerbe (2008) has written an excellent book using this approach, *Integrated Treatment of Eating Disorders: Beyond the Body Betrayed.* Again, this is a book for professionals but very accessible.

There is another very accessible book with a similarly integrative approach that is not explicitly about disordered eating, but about the emotional growth of young women: Mary Pipher (1995) *Reviving Ophelia: Saving the Selves of Adolescent Girls.* It's highly relevant to all the problems that have been discussed in this book.

There is one book which attempts to compare and contrast treatments for eating disorders by Miller and Mizes (2000), *Comparative Treatments of Eating Disorders.* It is a little out of date, but is very clear in conceptualising the differences between different treatment approaches and notes the growth of integrative approaches.

Understanding Your Eating: Courses for Emotional Eaters

If you have found this book useful and if you have come to the point of recognising that your eating may, at least in part, be driven by your feelings, you may find the courses delivered by Understanding your Eating useful. Have a look at the description that follows and if you are interested look it up on the internet: www.understandingyoureating.co.uk

The Understanding your Eating Programme has developed as a commercial programme out of research conducted by Professor Julia Buckroyd at the University of Hertfordshire. This group programme is designed to offer a publicly available resource for people who are aware that their overeating or compulsive eating is emotionally driven. It does not offer dieting or exercise advice or products, since it is based on the assumption that the vast majority of those who are overweight or suffer from disordered eating know what it is that they should be doing. The problem lies in doing it and in continuing to do it for the future. The literature on which the programme is based and an earlier form of the intervention is described in the book by Buckroyd and Rother (2007) *Therapeutic Groups for Obese Women*.

The programme has three parts. The first part is an introduction to the programme and consists of five seminars conducted weekly and lasting one and a half hours and also available on line. The seminars have the following titles:

- Seminar 1 – Eating is not just about Hunger
- Seminar 2 – Eating to Manage Feelings
- Seminar 3 – Self-esteem and How it Helps You Look After Yourself Better
- Seminar 4 – Improving Body Esteem
- Seminar 5 – Using People Instead of Food to Get You Through the Day.

The second part of the programme consists of nine free-standing modules of four weeks, each weekly seminar lasting one and a half hours also available on line. These modules which can be selected by participants according to choice, deal in greater depth with the material covered in the introductory seminars and have the following titles:

- Emotional Eating
- Feelings and Thoughts
- Motivation and Empowerment
- Food Monitoring
- Activity
- Self-nurture
- Relationships
- Self-esteem
- Body Esteem.

The third part of the programme offers support via email or telephone for those who have participated in at least the Introduction.

The first two parts of the programme are conducted in groups. The introduction has no more than 12 participants; the modules have no more than 10. Currently the support package is offered on an individual basis, but there are plans to develop internet support groups.

The programme was piloted from October 2007 to July 2008 at the University of Hertfordshire, but since August 2008 has been developed as a commercial project to be delivered at a range of different locations across the UK. For further detail see http://www.understandingyoureating.co.uk or contact Professor Julia Buckroyd, julia@juliabuckroyd. co.uk

Further Reading

American Psychiatric Association (APA) (2000) *Diagnostic and Statistical Manual of Mental Disorders DSM-IV-TR*, 4th edition. Washington, DC, APA.

Bass, E. and Davis, L. (1988) *The Courage to Heal: A Guide for Women Survivors of Child Sexual Abuse*. London, Vermilion.

Bass, E. and Davis, L. (2003) *Beginning to Heal: A First Book for Men and Women Who Were Sexually Abused as Children*. New York, HarperCollins.

Basso, M.J. (2003) *Underground Guide to Teenage Sexuality*, 2nd edn. Minneapolis, MN, Fairview Press.

Bowlby, J. (2000a) *Attachment*. London, Basic Books.

Bowlby, J. (2000b) *Separation*. London, Basic Books.

Bowlby, J. (2000c) *Loss*. London, Basic Books.

Bowlby, J. (2005) *The Making and Breaking of Affectional Bonds*. London, Routledge.

Bruch, H. (2001) *The Golden Cage: The Enigma of Anorexia Nervosa*. Cambridge, MA, Harvard University Press.

Bryant Jefferies, R. (2005) *Eating Disorders in Men*. Abingdon, Radcliffe.

Buckroyd, J. and Rother, S. (2007) *Therapeutic Groups for Obese Women*. Chichester, Wiley.

Buckroyd, J. and Rother, S. (eds.) (2008) *Psychological Responses to Eating Disorders and Obesity*. Chichester, Wiley.

Button, E. (1993) *Eating Disorders: Personal Construct Therapy and Change*. Chichester, Wiley.

Cash, T.F. (2008) *The Body Image Workbook: An Eight Step Programme for Learning to Like your Looks*, 2nd edn. Oakland, CA, New Harbinger.

Chernin, K. (1986) *The Hungry Self: Women, Eating and Identity*. London, Virago.

Conner, M. and Armitage, C.J. (2002) *The Social Psychology of Food*. Buckingham, Open University Press.

Cooper, M. and McLeod, J. (2010) *Pluralistic Counselling and Psychotherapy*. London, Sage.

Cooper, P. (2009) *Bulimia Nervosa and Binge Eating: A Self-help Guide Using Cognitive Behavioural Techniques*. London, Robinson.

Dokter, D. (ed.) (1994) *Arts Therapies and Clients with Eating Disorders*. London, Jessica Kingsley Publishers.

Fairburn, C. (1995) *Overcoming Binge Eating*. New York, Guilford Press.

Fairburn, C. (2008) *Cognitive Behaviour Therapy for Eating Disorders*. New York, Guilford Press.

Fairburn, C.G. and Bohn, K. (2005) Eating Disorder NOS (EDNOS): an example of the troublesome category 'not otherwise specified' (NOS) category in DSM-IV. *Behaviour Research and Therapy*, 43(6) 691–670.

Fairburn, C.G., Cooper, Z., Bohn, K., O'Connor, M., Doll, H. A. and Palmer, R.L. (2007) The severity and status of Eating Disorder NOS; Implications for DSM V, *Behaviour Research and Therapy*, 45(8), 1705–1715.

Gerhardt, S. (2004) *Why Love Matters: How Affection Shapes a Baby's Brain*. Hove, UK, Brunner Routledge.

Gilbert, S. (2000) *Counselling for Eating Disorders*. London, Sage.

Goleman, D. (1995) *Emotional Intelligence*. New York, Bantam.

Harris. T.A. (1995) *I'm OK – You're OK*. London, Arrow Books.

Hornyak, L. and Baker, E. (1989) *Experiential Therapies for Eating Disorders*. New York, Guilford Press.

Jacob, F. (2001) *Solution Focused Recovery from Eating Distress*. London, BT Press.

Kayrooz, C. (2001) *Systemic Treatment of Bulimia Nervosa*. London, Jessica Kingsley Publishers.

Langley, J. (2006) *Boys Get Anorexia Too: Coping with Male Eating Disorders in the Family*. London, Paul Chapman.

Lawrence, M. and Dana, M. (1990) *Fighting Food: Coping with Eating Disorders*. London, Penguin.

Leach, K. (2006) *The Overweight Patient: A Psychological Approach to Understanding and Working with Obesity*. London, Jessica Kingsley Publishers.

Lock, J., Agras, S., LeGrange, D. and Dare, C. (2002) *Treatment Manual for Anorexia Nervosa: A Family-based Approach*. New York, Guilford Press.

Logue, A.W. (2004) *The Psychology of Eating and Drinking*. New York, Brunner-Routledge.

Longhurst, A. (2003) *Body Confidence*. London, Michael Joseph.

McLeod, J. (2007) *Counselling Skill*. Maidenhead, Open University Press.

Miller, K. and Mizes, J.S. (2000) *Comparative Treatments of Eating Disorders*. London, Free Association Books.

Milos, G., Spindler, A., Schnyder, U. and Fairburn, C.G. (2005) Instability of eating disorder diagnoses: prospective study. *British Journal of Psychiatry*, 187, 573–578.

Morgan, J. (2008) *The Invisible Man: A Self-help Guide for Men with Eating Disorders, Compulsive Exercise and Bigorexia*. Hove, UK, Routledge.

National Institute of Health and Clinical Excellence (NICE) (2004) *Core Interventions in the Treatment and Management of Anorexia Nervosa, Bulimia Nervosa and Related Eating Disorders*. London, NICE.

National Institute of Health and Clinical Excellence (NICE) (2006) *Obesity: The Prevention, Identification, Assessment and Management of Overweight and Obesity in Adults and Children*. London, NICE.

Ogden, J. (2003) *The Psychology of Eating*. Oxford, Blackwell.

Orbach, S. (2010) *Bodies*. London, Profile Books.

Orford, J. (2001) *Excessive Appetites: A Psychological View of Addictions*, 2nd edn. Chichester, Wiley.

Paterson, A. (2004) *Fit to Die: Men and Eating Disorders*. Bristol, Lucky Duck.

Pipher, M. (1995) *Reviving Ophelia: Saving the selves of Adolescent Girls*. New York, Ballantine.

Prior, V. and Glaser, D. (2006) *Understanding Attachment and Attachment Disorders*. London, Jessica Kingsley Publishers.

Rabin, M. (2003) *Art Therapy and Eating Disorders: The Self as Significant Form*. New York, Columbia University Press.

Schmidt, U. and Treasure, J. (1997) *Getting Better Bit(e) by Bit(e): A Survival Kit for Sufferers of Bulimia Nervosa and Binge Eating Disorder*. Hove, UK, Psychology Press.

Schore, A.N. (2003) *Affect Regulation and the Repair of the Self*. New York, Norton.

Schwartz, M.F. and Cohn, L. (eds.) (1996) *Sexual Abuse and Eating Disorders*. Bristol, Brunner/Mazel.

Sroufe, L.A. (1995) *Emotional Development: The Organization of Emotional Life in the Early Years*. Cambridge, Cambridge University Press.

Treasure, J., Smith, G. and Crane, A. (2007) *Skills Based Learning for Caring for a Loved One with an Eating Disorder: The New Maudsley Method*. London, Routledge.

Vanderlinden, J. and Vandereycken, W. (1997) *Trauma, Dissociation and Impulse Dyscontrol in Eating Disorders*. Philadelphia, PA, Brunner/Mazel.

Wardle, A. (1997) *Consumption, Food and Taste*. London, Sage.

World Health Organisation (WHO) (1993) *The ICD-10 Classification of Mental and Behavioural Disorders*. Geneva, WHO.

Zerbe, K.J. (2008) *Integrated Treatment of Eating Disorders: Beyond the Body Betrayed*. New York, Norton.

Notes

Preface

1   If you would like to see what I have written, my publications are listed on my website: http://www.juliabuckroyd.co.uk.

2   There is a huge literature on attachment. What follows are just a few of the relevant references:

Bowlby, J. (2000a) *Attachment*. London, Basic Books.

Bowlby, J. (2000b) *Separation*. London, Basic Books.

Bowlby, J. (2000c) *Loss*. London, Basic Books. These are the key texts for attachment. Wonderful read and make a fantastic basis for thinking about later work.

Bowlby, J. (2005) *The Making and Breaking of Affectional Bonds*. London, Routledge. This is the short version if you are daunted by the three volumes.

Gerhardt, S. (2004) *Why Love Matters: How Affection Shapes a Baby's Brain*. Hove UK, Brunner Routledge. An easy introduction to attachment theory and infant development. She describes it as an accessible version of Allan Schore's work. This is a useful introduction to neuroscience and a very nice book.

Schore, A.N. (2003) *Affect Regulation and the Repair of Self*. New York, Norton. I consider Schore to be the real master in thinking about the relationship of attachment to emotional dysfunction. However, he is difficult to read. It helps if you know quite a lot before you start to read him.

Sroufe, L.A. (1995) *Emotional Development: The Organization of Emotional Life in the Early Years*. Cambridge, Cambridge University Press. Wonderful insights into child development.

Stern, D.N. (2000) *The Interpersonal World of the Infant*. New York, Basic Books. Lots about how mothers create the relationship with their child.

Introduction

1   American Psychiatric Association (APA) (2000) *Diagnostic and Statistical Manual of Mental Disorders DSM-IV-TRs*, 4th edn revised. Washington, DC, APA. This manual is very widely used as a means of diagnosing mental and emotional problems. Being diagnosable according to these criteria has often been the route to treatment, especially in the USA, but increasingly, also in the UK. A further version is expected in 2013.

2   Fairburn, C.G. and Bohn, K. (2005) Eating Disorder NOS (EDNOS): an example of the troublesome category 'not otherwise specified' (NOS) category in DSM-IV. *Behaviour Research and Therapy*, 43(6) 691–670.
    Fairburn, C.G., Cooper, Z., Bohn, K., O'Connor, M., Doll, H. A. and Palmer, R.L. (2007) The severity and status of Eating Disorder NOS; Implications for DSM V, *Behaviour Research and Therapy*, 45(8), 1705–1715.
    Milos, G., Spindler, A., Schnyder, U. and Fairburn, C.G. (2005) Instability of eating disorder diagnoses: prospective study. *British Journal of Psychiatry*, 187, 573–578.

Chapter 1

1   There are numerous sources of this information on the internet. Try http://www.patient.co.uk/about.asp. Also http://www.iotf.org/database/index.asp. which gives percentages broken down by district. The Dept of Health website is http://www.dh.gov.uk/en/Publichealth/Obesity/index.htm

2   The website of b-eat (the Eating Disorders Association, the leading charity for eating disorders in the UK) is very informative: http://www.b-eat.co.uk/ProfessionalStudentResources/Student information-1/SomeStatistics.

3   http://www.nhs.uk/Conditions/Binge-eating/Pages/Diagnosis.aspx is quite a useful website on binge eating.

Chua, J.L., Touyz, S. and Hill, A.J. (2004) Negative mood-induced overeating in obese binge eaters: an experimental study. *International Journal of Obesity and Related Metabolic Disorders*, 28:4, 606–610.

Freeman, L.M. and Gil, K.M. (2004) Daily stress, coping and dietary restraint in binge eating. *International Journal of Eating Disorders*, 36, 204–212.

Gluck, M. E., Geliebter, A. and Lorence, M. (2004) Cortisol stress response is positively correlated with central obesity in obese women with binge eating disorder (BED) before and after cognitive-behavioral treatment. *Annals of the New York Academy of Sciences*, 1032, 202–207.

Linde, J.A., Jeffrey, R.W., Levy, R.L., Sherwood, N.E., Utter, J., Pronk, N.P. and Boyle, R.G. (2004) Binge eating disorder, weight control self-efficacy, and depression in overweight men and women. *International Journal of Obesity and Related Metabolic Disorders*, 28:3, 418–425.

Yanovski, S.Z. (2003) Binge eating disorder and obesity in 2003: Could treating an eating disorder have a positive effect on the obesity epidemic? *International Journal of Eating Disorders*, 34, S117–S120.

4 Devlin, B., Bacanu, S.-A., Klump, K.L., Bulik, C.M., Fichter, M.M., Halmi, K.A., Kaplan, A.S., Strober, M., Treasure, J., Woodside, D.B., Berrettini, W.H. and Kaye, W.H. (2002) Linkage analysis of anorexia nervosa incorporating behavioral covariates. *Human Molecular Genetics*, 11(6), 689–696. Despite its intimidating title this is an interesting article and an example of how researchers have tried to investigate the subject.

5 Barness, L.A., Opitz, J.M. and Gilbert-Barness, E. (2007) Genetic, molecular and environmental aspects of obesity. *American Journal of Medical Genetics*, 143A(24), 3016–3034.

Bell, C.G., Walley, A.J. and Froguel, P. (2005) The genetics of human obesity. *Nature Reviews*, 6, 221–234.

6 See, for instance, http://www.hiddenlives.org.uk/articles/poverty.html. My mother claimed to have known about deaths

from starvation in the north east of England in the 1920s and 1930s.

7 See, for instance, this website which describes the waste of fruit crops for cosmetic reasons: http://www.foe.co.uk/resource/briefings/supermarket_british_fruit.pdf.

8 See, for instance, this report: http://news.bbc.co.uk/1/hi/uk/7389351.stm.

9 Logue, A.W. (2004) *The Psychology of Eating and Drinking*. New York, Brunner-Routledge.
Ogden, J. (2003). *The Psychology of Eating*. Oxford, Blackwell.

10 There is a wonderful book that I highly recommend on this whole subject of babies and what they need from their caregivers: Gerhardt, S. (2004) *Why Love Matters*. London, Routledge.

11 Gilbert, P. (2009) *The Compassionate Mind: A New Approach to Life's Challenges*. New York, New Harbinger.

12 This is the message of the attachment research quoted in note 2 at the end of the Preface.

13 These references are just a fraction of a large literature on this subject.
Felitti, V.J. (1991) Long-term medical consequences of incest, rape and molestation. *Southern Medical Journal*, 84(3), 328–331.
Felitti, V.J. (1993) Childhood sexual abuse, depression and family dysfunction in adult obese patients: a case control study. *Southern Medical Journal*, 86(7), 732–736.
Felitti, V.J., Anda, R.F., Nordenberg, D., Williamson, D.F., Spitz, A.M., Edwards, V., Koss, M.P. and Marks, J.S. (1998) Relationship of childhood abuse and household dysfunction to many of the leading causes of death in adults. *American Journal of Preventive Medicine*, 14, 245–258.
Frothingham, T.E., Hobbs, C.J., Wynne, J.M., Yee, L., Goyal, A. and Wadsworth, D.J. (2000) Follow-up study eight years after diagnosis of sexual abuse. *Archives of Disease in Childhood*, 83, 132–134.

Goodspeed Grant, P. and Boersma, H. (2005) Making sense of being fat: a hermeneutic analysis of adults' explanations for obesity. *Counselling and Psychotherapy Research*, 5(3), 212–220.

Grilo, C.M. and Masheb, R.M. (2001) Childhood psychological, physical and sexual maltreatment in outpatients with binge eating disorder: frequency and associations with gender, obesity and eating-related psychopathology. *Obesity Research*, 9, 320–325.

Grilo, C.M., Masheb, R.M., Brody, M., Toth, C., Burke-Martindale, C. and Rothschild, B. (2005) Childhood maltreatment in extremely obese male and female bariatric surgery candidates. *Obesity Research*, 13(1), 123–130.

Gustafson, T.B. and Sarwer, D.B. (2004) Childhood sexual abuse and obesity. *Obesity Reviews*, 5, 129–135.

Jia, H., Li, J.Z., Leserman, J., Hu, Y. and Drossman, D. (2004) Relationship of abuse history and other risk factors with obesity among female gastrointestinal patients. *Digestive Diseases and Sciences*, 49(5), 872–877.

Kendall-Tackett, K. (2002) The health effects of childhood abuse: four pathways by which abuse can influence health. *Child Abuse and Neglect*, 6(7), 715–730.

Kent, A., Waller, G. and Dagnan, D. (1999) A greater role of emotional than physical or sexual abuse in predicting disordered eating attitudes: the role of mediating variables. *International Journal of Eating Disorders*, 25(2), 159–167.

Sickel, A.E., Noll, J.G., Moore, P.J., Putnam, F.W. and Trickett, P.K. (2002) The long-term physical health and healthcare utilization of women who were sexually abused as children. *Journal of Health Psychology*, 7(5), 583–597.

Smolak, L. and Murnen, S.K. (2002) A meta-analytic examination of the relationship between child sexual abuse and eating disorders. *International Journal of Eating Disorders*, 31, 136–150.

Wonderlich, S.A., Crosby, R.D., Mitchell, J.E., Thompson, K.M., Redlin, J., Demuth, G., Smyth, J. and Haseltine, B. (2001) Eating disturbance and sexual trauma in childhood and adulthood. *International Journal of Eating Disorders*, 30, 401–412.

14 Schore, A.N. (2003) *Affect Regulation and the Repair of the Self*. New York, Norton.

15 Goleman, D. (1996) *Emotional Intelligence*. London, Bloomsbury. I heartily recommend this book. Goleman has a great deal to say about the subjects that are raised in this chapter and says it in a very accessible way.

16 Heinrichs, M., Baumgartner, T., Kirschbaum, C. and Ehlert, U. (2003). Social support and oxytocin interact to suppress cortisol and subjective responses to psychosocial stress. *Biological Psychiatry*, 54, 1389–1398.

17 Damasio, A.R. and Dolan, R.J. (1999) *The Feeling of What Happens: Body and Emotion in the Making of Consciousness*. Boston, MA, Harcourt.

18 Alexithymia is the technical name for having no (or not enough) words for feelings. Here is a sample of the research that demonstrates that it is a common problem for people with disordered eating.

De Zwaan, M., Bach, M., Mitchell, J.E., Ackard, D., Specker, S.M., Pyle, R.L. and Pakesch, G. (1995) Alexithymia, obesity and binge eating disorder. *International Journal of Eating Disorders*, 17, 135–140.

Pinaquy, S., Chabrol, H., Simon, C., Louvet, J.P. and Barbe, P. (2003) Emotional eating, alexithymia and binge eating disorder in obese women. *Obesity Research*, 11, 195–201.

Råstam, M., Gillberg, C., Gillberg, I.C. and Johansson, M. (1997) Alexithymia in anorexia nervosa: a controlled study using the 20-item Toronto Alexithymia Scale. *Acta Psychiatrica Scandinavia*, 95, 385–388.

Schmidt, U., Jiwany, A. and Treasure, J. (1993) A controlled study of alexithymia in eating disorders. *Comprehensive Psychiatry*, 34, 54–58.

19 Colantuoni, C., Rada, P., McCarthy, J., Patten, C., Avena, N.M., Chadeayne, A. and Hoebel, B. G. (2002) Evidence that intermittent, excessive sugar intake causes endogenous opioid dependency. *Behaviour Modification*, 27, 478–488.
Will, M. J., Franzblau, E. B. and Kelley, A. E. (2003) Neucleus accumbens mu-opioids regulate intake of a high-fat diet via activation of a distributed brain network. *Journal of Neuroscience*, 23, 2882–2888.
Will, M. J., Franzblau, E. B. and Kelley, A. E. (2004) The amygdala is critical for opioid-mediated binge eating of fat. *Neuroreport*, 15, 1857–1860.
Wonderlich, S.A., Crosby, R.D., Mitchell, J.E., Thompson, K.M., Redlin, J., Demuth, G., Smyth, J. and Haseltine, B. (2001) Eating disturbance and sexual trauma in childhood and adulthood. *International Journal of Eating Disorders*, 30, 401–412.
20 Dallman, M.F., Pecoraro, N.C. and la Fleur, S. E. (2005) Chronic stress and comfort foods: self-medication and abdominal obesity. *Brain, Behavior and Immunity*, 19, 275–280.
Epel, E., Lapidus, R., McEwen, B. and Brownell, K. (2001) Stress may add bite to appetite in women: a laboratory study of stress-induced cortisol and eating behaviour. *Psychoneuroendocrinology*, 26, 37–49.
Schoemaker, C., McKitterick, C.R., McEwen, B.S. and Kreek, M.J. (2002) Bulimia nervosa following psychological and multiple child abuse: support for the self-medication hypothesis in a population based cohort study. *International Journal of Eating Disorders*, 32, 381–388.

Chapter 2

1 Donald Winnicott is the grandfather of many of the ideas in this book. He was a paediatrician working in London and developed theories about the importance of the relationship between

mother and child that were radical for their time. You can get an idea of his work from a digest of his writing: Davis, M. and Wallbridge, D. (1981) *Boundary and Space: An Introduction to the Work of D.W. Winnicott*. London, Karnac.

2   Truby King's methods have aroused enormous controversy, equalled only by ongoing controversy about Claire Verity who promotes his methods in the UK, but was discredited for claiming qualifications she did not possess. You can follow the controversy on the internet by putting these names in the search engine.

3   Gina Ford is another who has followed Truby-King-like strategies and has aroused particularly violent responses from Mumsnet. You can follow this controversy online as well. Just put Gina Ford into the search engine.

4   Wardle, A. (1997) *Consumption, Food and Taste*. London, Sage. A fascinating sociological account of changing habits and taste in food in the UK.

5   The British Heart Foundation website http://www.heartstats.org gives comparative figures for different countries. The differences are startling.

Chapter 4

1   Bruch, H. (2001) *The Golden Cage: The Enigma of Anorexia Nervosa*. Cambridge, MA, Harvard University Press.

2   Wing, R.R. and Phelan, S. (2005) Long term weight loss maintenance. *American Journal of Clinical Nutrition*, 82(1), 222S–225S. This article suggests that about 20 per cent of those who undertake weight loss can maintain a clinically useful loss of 10 per cent or more of baseline weight for one year. That leaves 80 per cent of us who don't.

Chapter 5

1   This is a website supposedly for parents on how to talk to their teenagers about sex and sexuality, but equally suitable

for teenagers themselves: http://parentingteens.about.com/od/teensexuality/. If you enter teenage sexuality into your browser you'll find a long list of helpful sites.

A book you might look at is Basso, M.J. (2003) *Underground Guide to Teenage Sexuality*, 2nd edn. Minneapolis, MN, Fairview Press.

Chapter 6

1   Lawrence, M. and Dana, M. (1990) *Fighting Food: Coping with Eating Disorders*. London, Penguin.

Chapter 7

1   Orbach, S. (2006) *Fat is a Feminist Issue*. London, Arrow Books.
2   Chernin, K. (1994) *The Hungry Self*. London, Virago.

Chapter 8

1   Vanderlinden, J. and Vandereycken, W. (1997) *Trauma, Dissociation and Impulse Dyscontrol in Eating Disorders*. Philadelphia, PA, Brunner/Mazel. These researchers were among the first to take seriously the effects of trauma in childhood as a causative factor in eating disorders.

Chapter 9

What follows is an indication of a large literature:
1   Grilo, C.M. and Masheb, R.M. (2001) Childhood psychological, physical and sexual maltreatment in outpatients with binge eating disorder: frequency and associations with gender, obesity and eating-related psychopathology. *Obesity Research*, 9, 320–325.

2 Grilo, C.M., Masheb, R.M., Brody, M., Toth, C., Burke-Martindale, C. and Rothschild, B. (2005) Childhood maltreatment in extremely obese male and female bariatric surgery candidates. *Obesity Research*, 13(1), 123–130.

3 Gustafson, T.B. and Sarwer, D.B. (2004) Childhood sexual abuse and obesity. *Obesity Reviews*, 5, 129–135.

4 Hulme, P.A. (2004) Theoretical perspectives on the health problems of adults who experienced childhood sexual abuse. *Issues in Mental Health Nursing*, 25(4), 339–361.

5 King, T.K., Clark, M.M. and Pera, V. (1996) History of sexual abuse and obesity treatment outcome. *Addictive Behaviours*, 21(3), 283–290.

6 Smolak, L. and Murnen, S.K. (2002) A meta-analytic examination of the relationship between child sexual abuse and eating disorders. *International Journal of Eating Disorders*, 31, 136–150.

7 Vanderlinden, J. and Vandereycken, W. (1997) *Trauma, Dissociation and Impulse Dyscontrol in Eating Disorders*. Philadelphia, PA, Brunner/Mazel. These researchers were among the first to take seriously the effects of trauma in childhood as a causative factor in eating disorders.

8 Weiderman, M.W., Sansone, R.A. and Sansone, L.A. (1999) Obesity among sexually abused women: an adaptive function for some? *Women & Health*, 29(1), 89–100.

9 Wonderlich, S.A., Crosby, R.D., Mitchell, J.E., Thompson, K.M., Redlin, J., Demuth, G., Smyth, J. and Haseltine, B. (2001) Eating disturbance and sexual trauma in childhood and adulthood. *International Journal of Eating Disorders*, 30, 401–412.

Chapter 10

1 These issues are discussed in more detail in Gilbert, S.C. and Thompson, J.K. (2002) Body shame in childhood and adolescence. Relations to general psychological functioning

and eating disorders. In Gilbert, P. and Miles, J. (2002) *Body Shame, Conceptualisation, Research and Treatment.* Hove, UK, Brunner Routledge.

2   Cash, T.F. (2008) *The Body Image Workbook: An Eight Step Programme for Learning to Like your Looks.* Oakland, CA, New Harbinger.

3   Longhurst, A. (2003) *Body Confidence.* London, Michael Joseph.

Chapter 11

1   There are a number of resources that you may find useful that focus on disordered eating in men.

Men Get Eating Disorders Too is a UK charity dedicated to advancing the knowledge and understanding of the subject: http://www.mengetedstoo.co.uk

B-eat, the main eating disorders charity in the UK, formerly known as The Eating Disorders Association, has an excellent website which includes information on men and eating disorders. B-eat is the largest UK charity dealing with these issues.

Morgan, J. (2008) *The Invisible Man: A Self-help Guide for Men with Eating Disorders, Compulsive Exercise and Bigorexia.* Hove, UK, Routledge. This is by far the most helpful book.

Bryant Jefferies, R. (2005) *Eating Disorders in Men.* Abingdon, Radcliffe. This is a book for counsellors using the person centred approach. However, it consists largely of two very interesting extended case studies, one of a very overweight man and one of an anorexic man, which may be useful for you to read.

Langley, J. (2006) *Boys Get Anorexia Too: Coping with Male Eating Disorders in the Family.* The author is the mother of a boy who developed serious anorexia at the age of 12. It is a heartfelt account but also includes a lot of useful information and reflection on the experience.

Paterson, A. (2004) *Fit to Die: Men and Eating Disorders*. Bristol, Lucky Duck.

2   Hudson, J.I., Hiripi, E., Pope, H.G. and Kessler, R.C. (2007) The prevalence and correlates of eating disorders in the National Comorbidity Survey Replication. *Biological Psychiatry*, 61(3), 348–358.

3   www.malehealth.co.uk is an excellent website.

4   Pope, H., Olivardia, R., Gruber, A. and Borowiecki, J. (1999) Evolving ideals of male body image as seen through action toys. *International Journal of Eating Disorders*, 26, 65–72.

5   Russell, C.J and Keel, P.K. (2002) Homosexuality as a specific risk factor for eating disorders in men. *International Journal of Eating Disorders*, 31(3), 300–306.

6   Leit, R.A., Gray, J.J. and Pope, H.G. (2002) The media's representation of the ideal male body: a cause for muscle dysmorphia. *International Journal of Eating Disorders*, 31(3), 331–338.

Mosley, P.E (2009) Bigorexia: body building and muscle dysmorphia. *European Eating Disorders Review*, 17(3), 191–198.

Olivardia, R. (2001) Mirror, mirror on the wall, who's the largest of them all. The features and phenomenology of muscle dysmorphia. *Harvard Review of Psychiatry*, 9(5), 254–259.

Pope, H.G., Phillips, K.A., Olivardia, R. and Olivar, R. (2002) *The Adonis Complex: The Secret Crisis of Male Body Obsession*. New York, Simon and Schuster.

7   If you want to address some of the psychological issues relating to your eating behaviour, you may want to choose a male counsellor, or join a group of men. See Chapter 12 Resources for information on how to do that.

Index

abuse *see* child abuse, sexual abuse
achievement, competition over 136–7
adolescence 71; difficulties of growing up 97–113; self-concept 186–7; transition to adulthood 67–71; *see also* puberty
advice 212
Al-Ateen 158
Alcoholics Anonymous 150, 158
anger/rage 32, 83, 88, 92, 93; mother-daughter relationship 132–3, 138–9
anorexia 4, 8, 9, 10, 38, 63, 76, 115–28; difficulties in growing up 97–101, 109–13; genetic factors 13–14; message of 123–7; over-protective family 115–23; prevalence 13; response to sexual abuse 160–1, 166–7
appearance *see* body shape, size and weight
arts therapies 218–19
attachment 30, 67, 133, 137, 183, 193; consequences of a history of poor attachment 31–42, 83–5

babies: dependence on caregiver 23–5; early experiences of food 46–9; *see also* children
Bass, E. 159

B-eat (formerly the Eating Disorders Association) 157, 210, 214, 237
binge eating 8, 9, 10, 13, 41–2
body awareness 33–5, 39–41, 135
body image: female 179–82; male 197–9
'Body Journey' 191
body shape, size and weight 3, 10; anxiety about 83, 84, 177–91; lookism 135–6, 177–8; media pressures 86–7; professions requiring thinness 112
British Association for Counselling and Psychotherapy (BACP) 7, 210
Bruch, H. 86, 115
buddy 6–7, 211–14
bulimia 4, 8, 9, 10, 13, 63, 76, 110–11; emotional emptiness 148–57; self-assertion 126–7
bullying 38, 103, 107, 108, 200–1, 201–2

cardiac rehabilitation programme 203–4
caregivers 23–31, 44; inadequate 27–31, 133; teaching children about life management 23–7; *see also* attachment, fathers, mothers, parents
Cash, T. 189
Chernin, K. 129
child abuse 28, 29, 190; sexual *see* sexual abuse

239

STOP WORRYING
Get Your Life Back on
Track with CBT

Ad Kerkhof

ISBN (Paperback)
9780335242528
2010

eBook also available

This practical book will give you insight into the content, nature and seriousness of your worrying.

Key features:

- Supports and offers advice to worriers
- Contains Cognitive Behavioural Therapy exercises
- Provides guidance for professionals

www.openup.co.uk   OPEN UNIVERSITY PRESS
McGraw - Hill Education

PURSUIT OF PERFECT
Stop Chasing Perfection
and Discover the True Path
to Lasting Happiness

Tal Ben-Shahar

9780071629034 (Paperback)
2009

eBook also available

We're all labouring under our own and society's expectations to be perfect in every way-to look younger, to make more money, to be happy all the time. But according to Tal Ben-Shahar, the New York Times bestselling author of *Happier*, the pursuit of perfect may actually be the number-one internal obstacle to finding happiness.

Key features:

- Applies cutting-edge research in the field of positive psychology
- Provides exercises for self reflection
- Uses Time-Ins" to help rediscover what you really want out of life